Eleanor Roosevelt

These and other titles are included in The Importance
Of biography series:

Alexander the Great	Adolf Hitler
Muhammad Ali	Harry Houdini
Louis Armstrong	Thomas Jefferson
James Baldwin	Mother Jones
The Beatles	Chief Joseph
Clara Barton	Joe Louis
Charlemagne	Malcolm X
Napoleon Bonaparte	Thurgood Marshall
Julius Caesar	Margaret Mead
Rachel Carson	Golda Meir
Charlie Chaplin	Michelangelo
Cesar Chavez	Wolfgang Amadeus Mozart
Winston Churchill	John Muir
Cleopatra	Sir Isaac Newton
Christopher Columbus	Richard M. Nixon
Hernando Cortes	Georgia O'Keeffe
Marie Curie	Louis Pasteur
Charles Dickens	Pablo Picasso
Emily Dickinson	Elvis Presley
Amelia Earhart	Jackie Robinson
Thomas Edison	Norman Rockwell
Albert Einstein	Eleanor Roosevelt
Duke Ellington	Anwar Sadat
Dian Fossey	Margaret Sanger
Benjamin Franklin	Oskar Schindler
Galileo Galilei	John Steinbeck
Emma Goldman	Tecumseh
Jane Goodall	Jim Thorpe
Martha Graham	Mark Twain
Lorraine Hansberry	Queen Victoria
Stephen Hawking	Pancho Villa
Jim Henson	H. G. Wells

THE IMPORTANCE OF

Eleanor Roosevelt

by
Eileen Morey

Lucent Books, P.O. Box 289011, San Diego, CA 92198-9011

Library of Congress Cataloging-in-Publication Data

Morey, Eileen, 1923–
    The importance of Eleanor Roosevelt / by Eileen Morey.
        p.   cm.—(The importance of)
    Includes bibliographical references and index.
    Summary: A biography of the first wife of a president to
have a public life and career of her own, devoted to helping
others and working for peace.
    ISBN 1-56006-086-7 (alk. paper),
    1. Roosevelt, Eleanor, 1884–1962—Juvenile literature.
    2. Presidents' spouses—United States—Biography—Juvenile
literature.   [1. Roosevelt, Eleanor, 1884–1962.   2. First
ladies.]
I. Title.   II. Series.
E807.1.R48M67   1998
973.917'092—dc21   97-6789
[B]   CIP
                                                             AC

Copyright 1998 by Lucent Books, Inc., P.O. Box 289011,
San Diego, California, 92198-9011
Printed in the U.S.A.

Contents

Foreword

THE IMPORTANCE OF biography series deals with individuals who have made a unique contribution to history. The editors of the series have deliberately chosen to cast a wide net and include people from all fields of endeavor. Individuals from politics, music, art, literature, philosophy, science, sports, and religion are all represented. In addition, the editors did not restrict the series to individuals whose accomplishments have helped change the course of history. Of necessity, this criterion would have eliminated many whose contribution was great, though limited. Charles Darwin, for example, was responsible for radically altering the scientific view of the natural history of the world. His achievements continue to impact the study of science today. Others, such as Chief Joseph of the Nez Percé, played a pivotal role in the history of their own people. While Joseph's influence does not extend much beyond the Nez Percé, his nonviolent resistance to white expansion and his continuing role in protecting his tribe and his homeland remain an inspiration to all.

These biographies are more than factual chronicles. Each volume attempts to emphasize an individual's contributions both in his or her own time and for posterity. For example, the voyages of Christopher Columbus opened the way to European colonization of the New World. Unquestionably, his encounter with the New World brought monumental changes to both Europe and the Americas in his day. Today, however, the broader impact of Columbus's voyages is being critically scrutinized. *Christopher Columbus,* as well as every biography in The Importance Of series, includes and evaluates the most recent scholarship available on each subject.

Each author includes a wide variety of primary and secondary source quotations to document and substantiate his or her work. All quotes are footnoted to show readers exactly how and where biographers derive their information, as well as provide stepping stones to further research. These quotations enliven the text by giving readers eyewitness views of the life and times of each individual covered in The Importance Of series.

Finally, each volume is enhanced by photographs, bibliographies, chronologies, and comprehensive indexes. For both the casual reader and the student engaged in research, The Importance Of biographies will be a fascinating adventure into the lives of people who have helped shape humanity's past and present, and who will continue to shape its future.

IMPORTANT DATES IN THE LIFE OF ELEANOR ROOSEVELT

1884

Born to Elliott and Anna (Hall) Roosevelt in New York City.

1892

Mother dies; Eleanor and brothers live with Grandmother Hall.

1894

Father dies.

1899–1902

Attends Mlle. Souvestre's private school in London.

1902–1903

Makes debut; joins Junior League and Consumers' League. Works as volunteer in settlement house.

1905

Marries Franklin Roosevelt.

1906–1916

Bears six children: Anna (1906), James (1907), Franklin Jr. (1909—dies at seven months), Elliott (1910), Franklin Jr. (1914), John (1916).

1910

Franklin is elected to New York Senate; family moves to Albany in 1911.

1913

Franklin is appointed assistant secretary of the navy; family moves to Washington.

1917

Eleanor works at Red Cross canteen; helps organize Navy Red Cross and occupational therapy program for servicemen; persuades Red Cross to provide recreational facilities for servicemen.

1920

Joins League of Women Voters; reports national legislation to league.

1921

Franklin contracts infantile paralysis (polio).

1922

Eleanor joins Women's Trade Union League; becomes finance chairwoman of women's division of state Democratic Party; gives first political speech.

1924

Is chairwoman of committee that makes (unsuccessful) first attempt to present women's interests plank to Resolution Committee at National Democratic Convention.

1927

Begins teaching at Todhunter School.

1928

Franklin is elected governor of New York; they move back to Albany.

1932

Franklin is elected president; move back to Washington.

1933

Eleanor gives first press conference; sponsors Arthurdale.

1936

Begins to write "My Day."

1938

Attends Southern Conference for Human Welfare in Birmingham, Alabama.

1939

Resigns from Daughters of American Revolution to protest exclusion of Marian Anderson.

1941–1942

Works as assistant director of Office of Civilian Defense.

1942

Travels to England to assess role of British women in World War II.

1942–1943

Tours American military bases in South Pacific and Caribbean.

1945

Franklin dies; Eleanor accepts appointment to UN General Assembly by President Truman.

1946

Assigned to Commission for Human Rights; members elect her chairwoman.

1948

Presents Universal Declaration of Human Rights to UN Assembly for approval.

1950–1962

Hosts televison talk show *Passports of Mankind.*

1952–1962

Tours Belgium, Middle East, and Far East to study customs and to promote world peace.

1953

Works for American Association for the United Nations.

1955

Acts as delegate to World Federation of United Nations Associations.

1956

Campaigns for Adlai Stevenson for president.

1960

Works for Adlai Stevenson, and then for John F. Kennedy for president.

1961

President Kennedy appoints her to UN General Assembly, the board of the Peace Corps, and the Commission on the Status of Women.

1962

Dies at age seventy-eight in her apartment in New York City; buried in rose garden at Hyde Park.

1972

Eleanor Roosevelt Gallery and wing of the Franklin D. Roosevelt Library at Hyde Park dedicated.

1977

U.S. Congress authorizes Eleanor Roosevelt National Historic Site at Hyde Park.

A Woman of Accomplishment

Determine one's position, state it bravely and then act boldly.

—Eleanor Roosevelt

Until Franklin Roosevelt was elected president, presidential wives played a nonpolitical role, serving as hostesses of the White House, walking behind their husbands at affairs of state, and entertaining the wives of visiting dignitaries.

Eleanor Roosevelt was an innovator. The wife of the thirty-second president of the United States took an active role in her husband's job. She wrote a nationally syndicated daily newspaper column called "My Day" in which she described her life in Washington and gave her opinion on social reform topics. Eleanor held her own press conferences, which she used to encourage the careers of female reporters by inviting only women reporters to attend. She lectured in person around the country, on the radio, and later on television. Because her husband's polio-crippled legs made traveling difficult for him, she journeyed all over the nation and then reported to him the social, economic, and political conditions she had seen. She often suggested remedies that he sometimes accepted, yet always considered.

Always defending the downtrodden, Eleanor involved herself with civil and human rights, social and racial justice, feminism, refugee relocation, nuclear disarmament, and world peace. A member of several social reform and political organizations, she worked actively to support the groups' causes. Although her critics accused her of being a naive gadfly, her defenders respected her activism and her

Eleanor Roosevelt was the first president's wife to take an active part in political issues. She often was heavily criticized for doing so.

She Never Gave Up

In Eleanor Roosevelt *Blanche Wiesen Cook assesses the continuing appeal of Eleanor.*

"In many ways Eleanor Roosevelt remains a bellwether for our belief system. A woman who insists on her right to self-identity, a woman who creates herself over and over again, a woman of consummate power and courageous vision continues to challenge our sense of what is acceptable and what is possible. To this day, there is no agreement as to who Eleanor Roosevelt was, what she represented, or how she lived her life. Her friends and her detractors have made extravagant claims of goodness and mercy, foolishness and naiveté. She has acquired sainthood and been consigned to sinner status. She continues to haunt our memories and inspire our days, because she never gave up on life; she never stopped learning and changing. She worked to transform our world in behalf of greater dignity and more security for all people, for women and men in equal measure."

commitment to human welfare not only in the United States but in the world.

Although modest, even self-effacing at times, Eleanor became an influential figure in the Democratic Party, the Commission on the Status of Women, the Southern Conference for Human Welfare, the Peace Corps, and the United Nations. As chairman of the Human Rights Commission of the United Nations, she drove her committee to work long hours to draft the Universal Declaration of Human Rights, which "promised dignity, political influence, and economic security to all the people of this planet."[1] After approving the document, the delegates gave a standing ovation to the person most responsible for its composition, Eleanor Roosevelt.

Resisting all pleas from friends to slow her pace after her husband's death, Eleanor continued to take on a series of humanitarian causes. One Thanksgiving Day, after serving her children and her grandchildren a full holiday dinner, Eleanor looked apologetically around the table and asked her family to excuse her. She had not quite finished packing for her trip to India, she told them, and she would be leaving in just a few hours. On her seventieth birthday she paused long enough to say, "Life has got to be lived!"[2]

Until her death at age seventy-eight, Eleanor traveled the world—sometimes as

Eleanor Roosevelt poses along with dozens of schoolchildren. Eleanor always took an interest in the lives of children—and their families.

a goodwill ambassador for subsequent U.S. presidents, sometimes as a volunteer—working for human rights and world peace. Although Eleanor never received the Nobel Peace Prize, in 1961 and again in 1962, nine months before her death, several prominent Americans, including Adlai Stevenson, Harry Truman, and John Kennedy, recommended that she be so honored. In his letter to Gunnar Jahn, chairman of the selection committee, Stevenson wrote, "In this tragic generation [she] has become a world symbol of the unity of mankind and the hope of peace."[3] The committee was not persuaded. At her funeral, which was attended by two former presidents, the current president, and one future president, former president Truman called her "First Lady of the World."[4]

How does one measure the importance of Eleanor Roosevelt? Count the troops of servicemen and -women she visited overseas during World War II? Total the thousands of miles she traveled in her efforts to improve the conditions for hu-

mankind? Ask for letters of recommendation from the heads of state whose countries she helped? Talk with the coal miners, the unemployed, the hungry, the oppressed, the homeless, or the prisoners in concentration camps to whom she listened so intently and took actions to help? Canvass the women—young and old and in between—whom she inspired during her lifetime and still inspires?

How did Eleanor rate her importance? On a trip for the United Nations, her companion, Dr. David Gurewitsch, pointed through the plane window to a huge crowd gathered at the airport. "Look!" he said.

"That's not for us," she replied. "Someone important must be flying in."[5]

When the two deplaned, the crowd surged forward. They had come to see her.

Eleanor used her position as first lady to advance the causes she championed, and in so doing, she was frequently cited as the most important woman of her time. Now many call her the most important woman of the century.

Chapter 1

Eleanor's Painful Childhood

I was very tall, very thin, and very shy.
—Eleanor Roosevelt

Eleanor Roosevelt began her autobiography by writing, "My mother was one of the most beautiful women I have ever seen."[6] A woman who measured success by a woman's beauty and social graces, Anna Hall Roosevelt found Anna Eleanor, born October 11, 1884, an eternal disappointment. Even in front of guests, Anna called her daughter "Granny," a nickname that caused Eleanor to blush and hang her head in shame. How could such a plain child ever uphold the family's position in New York society—a concern of prime importance to Anna. After all, she and her husband, Elliott, were the popular leaders of New York City's young high society set. Apparently seeing no value in her daughter, Anna once told her, "You have no looks, so see to it that you have manners."[7]

However, Eleanor's father, good-looking Elliott Roosevelt, loved her completely and doted on her. When he came home in the evening, he would pick her up and swing her around, much to her delight. Her day and her life revolved around him.

Elliott was cross with Eleanor only when she would show fear, which unfortunately she often did. She never forgot an incident that happened during a family visit to Italy:

> We went to Sorrento and I was given a donkey so I could ride over the beautiful roads. One day the others overtook me and offered to let me go with them, but at the first steep descent which they slid down, I turned pale

Eleanor's mother, Anna Hall Roosevelt (pictured), was continually disappointed by her daughter's gawky looks, making no secret of the fact that she felt Eleanor a lost cause.

and preferred to stay on the high road. I can remember still the tone of disapproval in my father's voice.[8]

The first four years of Eleanor's life were typical for the daughter of a well-to-do young couple. As was the custom in wealthy families of the late 1800s, a French nurse cared for baby Eleanor from her infancy and into her early childhood and took over her early education. The nurse taught her both French and English.

Her World Collapses

Eleanor was only four years old when her world foundered with her father's physical and emotional breakdown:

Whether it was some weakness from his early years, whether it was the pain he endured from a broken leg which had to be set, rebroken and reset, I do not know. My father began to drink, and my mother, his sisters, and his brother, Theodore, began the period of harrowing anxiety which was to last until his death in 1894.[9]

Besides drinking, Elliott was taking morphine and laudanum, which were prescribed freely in the 1880s to control pain.

After the birth of Eleanor's brother, Elliott Jr., in 1889, Eleanor's father went to Bermuda for a few weeks to try to get his drinking under control. He failed. In the summer of 1890, Elliott, Anna, and the children sailed to Europe in search of a sanitarium that could help Elliott. He was

Victorian Standards

Eleanor knew early the kind of life she was supposed to have, as she describes in volume one of her autobiography, This Is My Story.

"My mother belonged to that New York City society which thought itself all-important. Old Mr. Peter Marié, who gave choice parties and whose approval stamped young girls and young matrons a success, called my mother a queen, and bowed before her charm and beauty, and to her this was important.

In that society you were kind to the poor, you did not neglect your philanthropic duties, you assisted the hospitals and did something for the needy. You accepted invitations to dine and dance with the right people only, you lived where you would be in their midst. You thought seriously about your children's education, you read the books that everybody read, you were familiar with good literature. In short, you conformed to the conventional pattern."

The Roosevelt family in a photo taken around 1892. From left to right are Elliott, Hall, Eleanor's father, and Eleanor.

first admitted to a sanitarium in Germany, but he kept escaping to get drunk. In the fall the family traveled to Italy to spend the winter sightseeing. Eleanor was happy because she was with her father every day.

A Move to France

In the spring the family moved to France, where Elliott entered another sanitarium. Anna settled into a house outside Paris with the two children. Since Anna was expecting her third child in June, Elliott's older sister, Anna, called Bamie by family and friends, came to help them.

Anna enrolled Eleanor in a convent school to improve her French, but Eleanor believed that her mother's motive was more "to have me out of the way when the baby arrived."[10] The convent, the nuns, the girls, their religion—all were strange to six-year-old Eleanor. The other girls would have nothing to do with her. She remembered later, "I longed to be allowed to join them, but was always kept on the outside and wandered by myself in the walled-in garden."[11] When one of her classmates became the center of attention one day after accidentally swallowing a coin, Eleanor made a bid for the spotlight by claiming that she too had swallowed a coin. The nuns quickly determined that Eleanor was lying and sent her home in disgrace. Her shame did not prevent her from lying occasionally to get the attention she craved.

After Eleanor's second brother, Hall, was born in June 1891, Anna wanted to go home to New York. Elliott had continued to sneak out of the sanitarium to go on long drinking bouts. Leaving him in France at the sanitarium, Anna and the children sailed for home. Her brother-in-law Theodore took over the reins of the family and ordered Elliott to stay away for two years unless he controlled his alcoholism. Still drinking, Elliott returned to the states, moved to Virginia, and organized a land development project for his

Following his brother's breakdown, Theodore Roosevelt took charge of Anna and the children until Elliott could get control of his alcoholism.

brother-in-law Douglas Robinson, husband of his sister Corrinne. He and Eleanor exchanged long, affectionate letters.

The next year, in October 1892, just before Eleanor's eighth birthday, Anna went into the hospital for undisclosed surgery. While recuperating, she became ill with diphtheria. Eleanor later recalled what happened next: "I can remember standing by a window when Aunt Susie [Mrs. Parish] told me that my mother was dead. This was on December 7, 1892. Death meant nothing to me, and one fact wiped out everything else. My father was back and I would see him soon."[12]

The Children Live with Grandmother Hall

Mindful of her husband's continuing alcoholism, Anna had not trusted Elliott to rear their three children. In her will she had left instructions that they live with her mother. Elliott did not come home after all, but he and Eleanor continued to correspond.

Grandmother Hall took the children in not only because her daughter had requested that she do so but also because she loved them. Wanting to help them, she decided that they should have what her own children had not had—discipline. "We were brought up on the principle that 'no' was better than 'yes,'"[13] Eleanor remembered.

In 1893 both of Eleanor's brothers, Ellie and Hall, became ill with scarlet fever. Baby Hall recovered, but three-year-old Ellie developed diphtheria and died.

Almost nine years old, Eleanor's only companion was her brother Hall. To ease

A Guilty Conscience

In Autobiography *Eleanor tells of a childhood escapade that troubled her young conscience.*

"My young aunts and their friends talked all the time of plays which I never went to see. As a result, one winter I committed a crime which weighed heavily on my conscience for a long time.

My grandmother told me to go to a charity bazaar with a friend. To escape my maid, I told her my friend would have her maid with her and that she would bring me home. Instead of going to the bazaar we went to see a play, *Tess of the D'Urbervilles*, which was being discussed by my elders and which I, at least, did not understand at all. We sat in the peanut gallery and were miserable for fear of seeing someone we knew. We left before the end because we knew we would be late in reaching home. I had to lie and could never confess, which I would gladly have done because of my sense of guilt, but I would have involved the other girl in my trouble."

her loneliness, Elliott sent her gifts: a kitten, a puppy, a pony. Sometimes he came to New York to see her. For Eleanor, the time between his visits was too long:

> Subconsciously I must always have been waiting for his visits. They were irregular, and he rarely sent word before he arrived, but never was I in the house, even in my room two long flights of stairs above the entrance door that I did not hear his voice the minute he entered the front door. Walking downstairs was far too slow. I slid down the banisters and usually catapulted into his arms before his hat was hung up.[14]

Then he began coming to New York, but avoiding his children. He explained to Mrs. Hall that he was just too depressed to see even Eleanor. In the summer of 1894, drunk as usual, he fell, slipped into unconsciousness, and died. Eleanor was not quite ten.

Having become the sole guardian of the children, Grandmother Hall tried to give Eleanor the education that Anna would have wanted her daughter to have. Eleanor studied with a private tutor in a friend's home. Eleanor took piano lessons and practiced faithfully although she had no musical talent. She enjoyed her ballet classes, but ballroom dancing classes were torture for her. She liked the dancing, but she hated the clothes she had to wear. The other girls wore dresses well below their knees at the dancing class, but Grandmother Hall made Eleanor wear dresses

Young Eleanor during the period when she was living with her grandmother. With her mother dead, and her father only visiting infrequently, Eleanor grew up without her parents' guidance.

above her knees with long black stockings and high-button shoes—all of which accented her height. Besides being tall and thin, Eleanor had developed the two physical features that would henceforth be her trademarks—a small, receding chin and prominent teeth.

Eleanor came nearest to being happy during the summer months when Grandmother Hall took her two sons, Eddie and Vallie, and two daughters, Pussie (Edith) and Maude, all grown but still living at home, and young Eleanor and Hall to Oak Terrace, her country home that overlooked the Hudson River. Eleanor and her Aunt Pussie would row a small boat five

miles down the river to Tivoli, the nearest town, get the mail, and row back for breakfast. Eleanor rode her pony, and with Uncle Vallie's help she learned how to jump with the pony. Sometimes the family had picnics and took carriage rides. For many hours, though, Eleanor had no one but Hall for company. Fortunately she loved to read, and Grandmother Hall's library was open to her. Eleanor's favorite place to read was in a cherry tree, which was a convenient place when she happened to choose a book of which her grandmother would not approve.

In 1898, when Eleanor was fourteen, she was invited to the home of her Aunt

Corrinne, her father's sister, for a Christmas party. The other girls wore long gowns; Eleanor wore a blue dress with a bow on each shoulder—and a hem above her knees. She was miserable all evening. She recalled the occasion years later: "I knew, of course, that I was different from all the other girls and if I had not they were frank in telling me so! I still remember my gratitude to my cousin Franklin Roosevelt when he came and asked me to dance with him."[15]

Later her Aunt Edith, Uncle Theodore's wife, wrote to Auntie Bye, "Poor little soul, she is very plain. Her mouth and teeth seem to have no future. But the ugly duckling may turn out to be a swan."[16]

Eleanor Goes to Allenswood

Knowing that Anna would have wanted her daughter to be educated abroad, Grandmother Hall sent fifteen-year-old Eleanor to Marie Souvestre's exclusive Allenswood School just outside London. On the ocean voyage Eleanor was chaperoned by her Aunt Tissie (Elizabeth Hall Mortimer), who had been living in England for

Studying with Souvestre

Eleanor loved almost every aspect of life at Allenswood, but she especially loved her classes with Souvestre, as she describes in Autobiography.

"Mlle. Souvestre held her history classes in her library, a charming and comfortable room lined with books and filled with flowers. We sat on little chairs on either side of the fireplace. Mlle. Souvestre carried a long pointer in her hand, and usually a map hung on the wall. She would walk up and down, lecturing to us. We took notes, but were expected to do a good deal of independent reading and research. We wrote papers on the subjects assigned and labored hard over them. This was the class we enjoyed beyond any other.

A few of us were occasionally invited in the evening to Mlle. Souvestre's study, and those were red-letter days. She had a great gift for reading aloud and she read to us, always in French, poems, plays and stories. If the poems were those she liked, occasionally she read them over two or three times and then demanded that we recite them to her in turn. I found this an exhilarating way to spend an evening."

Eleanor (above) at fifteen, the age at which she attended Allenswood School. Eleanor (top row, center) found a new sense of belonging at the school, especially when Mlle. Souvestre became the young woman's mentor.

several years with her artist husband, Stanley. Aunt Tissie would broaden her niece's education during school breaks by taking her to various places in Europe and by introducing her to people of different nationalities, backgrounds, and occupations.

When Eleanor met Marie Souvestre, the master teacher looked into Eleanor's blue eyes and sensed her new student's unplumbed potential. Freed from her grandmother's restraints, Eleanor began to blossom almost immediately. She was delighted to learn that the girls wore a uniform—white blouses, dark ankle-length skirts, and straw hats. Nobody would make fun of her clothes. All of the girls had to speak French, but Eleanor had been bilingual from the time she learned to talk. Even the strict rules—only three ten-minute baths a week, a long brisk walk after breakfast every day regardless of the weather, frequent room inspections—were no problem for Eleanor. She settled in with a sense of belonging that she had never known before.

A Strong Sense of Duty

In This Is My Story, *Eleanor tells us how she developed her sense of duty, which as an adult she considered her strongest trait.*

"Very early I became conscious of the fact that there were people around me who suffered in one way or another. I was five or six when my father took me to help serve Thanksgiving dinner in one of the newsboys' clubhouses. My father explained that many of these ragged little boys had no homes and lived in little wooden shanties in empty lots, or slept in vestibules of houses or public buildings or any place where they could be moderately warm, yet they were independent and earned their own livings.

Every Christmas I was taken by my grandmother to help dress the Christmas tree for the babies' ward in the Post-Graduate Hospital."

Eleanor was soon invited to sit at Souvestre's table in the dining room, a sure sign of approval. The headmistress somehow managed to have favorites without offending the other girls, and Eleanor became her most favorite. At the dining table Eleanor developed a habit that helped her for the rest of her life:

Frequently I would use, in talking with Mlle. Souvestre, things which I had overheard in her conversations with her friends and which had passed through my rather quick mind, giving me some new ideas; but if anyone had asked me any questions he would soon have discovered that I had no real knowledge of the thing I was talking about.

More and more, as I grew older, I used the quickness of my mind to pick the minds of other people and use their knowledge as my own. Few people were aware how little I actually knew on a variety of subjects I talked about with apparent ease.

This is a bad habit, but it gives you a facility in picking up information about a great variety of subjects.[17]

Eleanor was a good student in most of her classes, excellent in language and literature. She worked hard for Souvestre, an exciting teacher who demanded that her students think.

Gradually gaining self-confidence, Eleanor lost most of her fears. She even stopped biting her nails. Gracious and kind to all of her classmates, she became one of the most popular girls in school. She stopped lying because she did not need to lie anymore: She was basking in attention from her classmates, her teachers, and most of all, Souvestre.

Eleanor spent part of the school holidays with Aunt Tissie and Uncle Stanley, who introduced her to London and to Europe. Later Souvestre invited Eleanor to travel with her, an experience that Eleanor would always treasure. Eleanor was in charge of all the details of their trips—making reservations, buying tickets, finding accommodations. Sometimes Souvestre let Eleanor explore a new city all by herself without a chaperone, a practice that horrified Grandmother Hall when she heard about it. Souvestre taught Eleanor to travel easily with enjoyment, to change the itinerary if she wanted, to eat native foods, to meet and talk with new people.

At the close of her third year at Allenswood, Eleanor wanted desperately to attend for a fourth year. Besides loving her life there, she knew that Souvestre, who was in her seventies, would not be teaching much longer. Eleanor recognized even then that Souvestre had been more than a teacher: She had been a mentor. But Eleanor would be eighteen in October, the age at which wealthy young girls in America were presented to society at formal balls. A life of parties and teas and dances did not appeal to Eleanor, but Grandmother Hall was adamant: Eleanor must come home.

2 The Emergence of Eleanor

I had painfully high ideals and a tremendous sense of duty.

—Eleanor Roosevelt

When Eleanor returned home in the late spring of 1902, she was already beginning to dread her December debut, her introduction to society. After the grand Assembly Ball in December, at which she and the other debutantes would be presented to the upper-class society of New York City, eighteen-year-old Eleanor would spend the rest of the winter going to teas, formal dinners, and dances. At least she would have the right clothes for those affairs because Aunt Tissie had helped her choose some while she was at Allenswood. Aunt Tissie had even ordered a stylish white gown from Paris for Eleanor to wear to the Assembly Ball.

Eleanor Debuts

During the summer Eleanor's old fear of failure returned to haunt her. Her grandmother, her mother, and her aunts had all been the popular beauties, the belles, of their debutante seasons; Eleanor was convinced that she would be the wallflower of hers. As far as the Assembly Ball was con-

cerned, she was right: "I went home early, thankful to get away. I knew I was the first girl in my mother's family who was not a belle and, though I never acknowledged it to any of them at that time, I was deeply ashamed."[18]

Eleanor in a photo taken in Switzerland in 1900. Eleanor's grandmother insisted that Eleanor quit school and return home so that she could "come out"—a ritual expected of all debutantes.

From an early age, Eleanor showed the resolve and bravery for which she would become well known. While other debutantes fulfilled their charitable obligations with fund-raisers, Eleanor taught classes to immigrant children in the slums of New York.

Eleanor fared better at the teas and dinners. As soon as hostesses learned that she was an interesting conversationalist, her invitations multiplied. Her ability to listen and to recall what she had heard served her well on those occasions. She made some new friends, and occasionally she would run into her fifth cousin, Franklin Roosevelt, one of the few young men she knew who was taller than she. Nearly six feet tall, Eleanor was self-conscious about her height.

Before Eleanor's debutante season had ended, Grandmother Hall decided to sell her house in New York City and live year-round in her country home. Eleanor moved in with her cousin Susie Parish and her family, so that she could continue to live in New York City and finish her year of parties.

One of the debutantes' responsibilities was to join the Junior League, a group of young women who did charitable works. Eleanor elected to work in the slums, an unusual choice for a debutante. She and her friend Jean Reid taught classes to the children of Jewish and Italian immigrants in the Remington Street Settlement House on New York's Lower East Side. Jean, a pianist, accompanied Eleanor, who taught social dancing and calisthenics.

Although Jean quite properly traveled to and from the settlement house in her parents' carriage as a debutante should, Eleanor defied custom and rode either the elevated railway or the Fourth Avenue streetcar. Walking in the dark from the settlement house to board the streetcar was a scary experience:

> The dirty streets, crowded with foreign-looking people, filled me with terror, and I often waited on a corner for a car, watching, with a great deal of trepidation, men come out of the saloons or shabby hotels nearby, but the children interested me enormously.[19]

They interested her enough that she continued to teach them for several months, and she continued to ride the streetcar. She would always prefer public transportation to private carriages, despite her family's disapproval.

In 1903 Eleanor joined the Consumers' League, which was dedicated to improving conditions for laborers, especially women, in garment factories and department stores. The league struggled to improve working conditions, which included bad lighting and ventilation, inadequate restroom facilities, primitive sanitary conditions, and one-dollar-a-day pay for a twelve-hour day six days a week. The league publicized the wretched working conditions in newspapers and speeches. It also appealed to government officials to enact laws to improve the situation. Eleanor accompanied an experienced investigator on visits to factories and stores and saw firsthand the dreadful conditions the women worked in. "It had never occurred to me that the girls might get tired standing behind counters all day long, or that no seats were provided for them if they had time to sit down and rest."[20]

Eleanor's family disapproved of her social reform work and tried to dissuade her from continuing it. Fearing that Eleanor might catch some horrible disease or be harmed in some way, Cousin Susie was particularly distressed. According to biographer Blanche Wiesen Cook, "Cousin Susie could see no reason for or benefit from Eleanor's efforts."[21] Eleanor was indeed shocked by what she was seeing, but she believed that she was doing something to improve some people's lives, a cause to which she would commit herself for the rest of her life.

Eleanor Dates Franklin Delano Roosevelt

Eleanor did not devote all of her time to settlement work and social reform, however. Riding the train to Grandmother Hall's home at Tivoli one day, she happened to meet Franklin Roosevelt. He took her into the next railroad car to meet his mother, Sara Delano Roosevelt, and the three of them talked until Franklin and his

mother got off the train at Hyde Park. Afterwards, the two young people saw each other occasionally at dinner parties.

Eventually they started seeing each other on their own, although Eleanor was always properly chaperoned by her maid or a relative. Franklin invited Eleanor to weekend parties at his family home in Hyde Park and his mother's summer home on Campobello Island off the coast of New Brunswick, Canada. In November 1903 he invited her to the Harvard-Yale football game. Sometime during the weekend they managed to elude Eleanor's chaperone for a while, and Franklin asked Eleanor to marry him. She accepted.

Opposite Personalities

Franklin was attracted to Eleanor's serious manner, and she certainly was almost always serious. As she recalled years later, "I had painfully high ideals and a tremendous sense of duty entirely unrelieved by any sense of humor or any appreciation of the weakness of human nature. Things were either right or wrong to me."[22] Franklin, good-looking, fun loving, and lighthearted, had a quick sense of humor and enjoyed being with people. Although opposites in personality, they did share one trait: Both Roosevelts had an inborn sense of duty.

When they told Franklin's mother about their intention, she was aghast. She had thought that they were just friends. Since the death of her husband, Sara had dedicated herself to her son, and she had no plans to step aside for a daughter-in-law. She did not object to Eleanor herself, for

Dating

Eleanor described the rules of dating in the early 1900s in This Is My Story.

"It was understood that no girl was interested in a man or showed any liking for him until he had made all the advances. There were few men who would have dared to use my first name, and to have signed oneself in any other way than 'very sincerely yours' would have been not only a breach of good manners but an admission of a feeling which was entirely inadmissible.

You never allowed a man to give you a present except flowers or candy or possibly a book. To receive a piece of jewelry from a man to whom you were not engaged was a sign of being a fast woman, and the idea that you would permit any man to kiss you before you were engaged to him never even crossed my mind."

Eleanor and Franklin at his estate in Hyde Park, New York, in a photo taken before they were married.

who could object to a Roosevelt? And Eleanor's father had been Franklin's godfather. Nonetheless, she insisted that for one year they keep their engagement a secret.

Franklin felt guilty enough about making a break with his mother that he told her, "I know what pain I must have caused you and you know I wouldn't do it if I really could have helped it."[23]

During the year of the secret engagement, Sara made determined efforts to keep the couple apart. She took Franklin on a six-week Caribbean cruise, during which he enjoyed a couple of light flirtations—encouraged by Sara. She tried to get her friend Joseph Choate, U.S. ambassador to England, to take Franklin with him as his secretary. Since Choate already had a secretary, he refused. Throughout the separation enforced by Sara, Eleanor and Franklin exchanged daily, long, affectionate letters.

Eleanor and Franklin Marry

In June 1904 Sara and Eleanor went with several of Franklin's cousins to Franklin's Harvard commencement, after which he enrolled in law school at Columbia University in New York City. Undeterred by Sara's tactics, they announced their engagement on December 1, 1904. They had to juggle their wedding date around Uncle Ted's—now President Theodore Roosevelt's—schedule, for he had agreed to give the bride away. Because the president would be in New York for the St. Patrick's Day celebration on March 17, 1905, Eleanor and Franklin set that date for their marriage. At the reception after the wedding, Franklin was surprised and a little annoyed when so many people congratulated him on winning Eleanor—and nobody congratulated her for catching him!

The newlyweds had two honeymoons, the first being a week at Sara's Hyde Park mansion. Then Franklin had to return to Columbia University to finish the term at law school. In June the couple went on a three-month tour of Europe. While they were gone, Sara rented and furnished a townhouse just three blocks from her home in New York City, and she hired a butler, a maid, and a cook for them.

Sara Delano Roosevelt and Eleanor at Campobello Island in 1903. From the start, the two had a strained relationship; they were destined to battle over who had control over Franklin and his family.

Eleanor in her wedding dress, after her marriage on March 17, 1905.

Until their house was ready, Eleanor and Franklin lived with Sara. Eleanor worked hard to become a model daughter-in-law, but Sara treated her as an interloper. A comfortable chair sat on either side of the fireplace, one for Sara and one for Franklin. Eleanor was supposed to sit anywhere else. When they ate their meals, Sara sat at the head of the table; Franklin, at the other end. Eleanor sat on one side, as a guest would.

For the decade from 1906 to 1916, Eleanor assumed a new role: "For ten years I was always just getting over having a baby or about to have one, and so my occupations were considerably restricted."[24] In 1906 she gave birth to Anna; 1907, James; 1909, Franklin Jr., who died at seven months; 1910, Elliott; 1914, Franklin Jr.; 1916, John. As a mother, Eleanor had

problems: "I had never had any interest in dolls or little children, and I knew absolutely nothing about handling or feeding a baby."[25] Instead of aiding Eleanor, Sara took charge. She hired a trained nurse to help with infant care for each baby and a succession of governesses to care for the children when they got older—all of whom answered to Sara, not Eleanor. Later Sara would tell the children, "I was your real mother, Eleanor merely bore you."[26] Since Franklin was not interested in domestic issues, Eleanor found herself dominated by Sara.

In 1908 life with Sara became even more trying. She hired an architect to design two identical townhouses, side by side, connected on one floor by sliding doors. Sara moved into one side; Franklin, Eleanor, Anna, and James moved into the other side. Eleanor never knew when Sara would sail through the sliding doors into the family's quarters.

Eleanor hardly seems to notice the scenery while in Venice on her honeymoon in 1905.

A photo of Eleanor's young family shows (from left to right) Elliott, Eleanor, Franklin, Franklin Jr., James, John (on Sara's lap), and Anna. The fact that Sara appears in this family photo is a testament to how she inserted herself into Eleanor's daily affairs.

Eleanor was not the only one who was finding life confining, however. Franklin, who had long envied the success of his cousin Theodore, had become bored with being a lawyer. Some leaders of the New York Democratic Party were searching for a candidate from Franklin's county to run for the state senate. The personable young Roosevelt appealed to the committee, especially since he could afford to finance his own campaign. Ed Perkins, Democratic county chairman, offered the candidacy to Franklin, who answered that he would have to talk with his mother. Perkins parked his car in front of the Poughkeepsie bank, where the other members of the committee waited to meet Franklin. Perkins said, "Frank, the men that are looking out of that window are waiting for your answer. They won't like to hear that you had to ask your mother."[27]

Franklin accepted the nomination and financed his own campaign. Driving a red Maxwell car to impress the voters, Franklin campaigned in almost every village in his Republican district—and won on the Democratic ticket.

They Move to Albany

Much to Eleanor's relief, she and Franklin and their children left Sara at Hyde Park when they moved to Albany, the state capital, in 1911. Away from Sara's dominance,

The indomitable Sara Delano Roosevelt was used to having a firm grip over her son, Franklin. Sara expected this control to continue after Franklin married.

Eleanor soon began to assert herself again. She entertained Franklin's political friends and called on their wives. She occasionally went to the gallery in the Capitol Building and listened to the speakers. Eleanor later defined her new role: "Here in Albany began for the first time a dual existence for me, which was to last all the rest of my life. Public service, whether my husband was in or out of office, was to be a part of our daily life from now on."[28]

Blanche Wiesen Cook, in the first volume of her biography of Eleanor, assesses her emergence as a political activist:

> She met with people in their homes, and lobbied for causes. She encouraged debate and never avoided disagreement. Listening to all those conversations between her aunt [Auntie Bye, Theodore's sister] and Uncle Theodore, ER had absorbed information and style. FDR appreciated ER's opinions. He listened to her ideas, and trusted her insights about her colleagues. He appreciated from the first that she was one of his biggest assets. She built bridges, even over the most treacherous terrain; she made what might have seemed impossible alliances.[29]

When the New York Democratic Party split into two factions in 1911, Eleanor retained the respect of both groups, and she convinced Franklin that he needed the endorsement of a united party if he was to succeed.

Franklin took Eleanor to Baltimore in June 1912 for their first Democratic National Convention. While he worked enthusiastically behind the scenes to nominate Woodrow Wilson, she watched the proceedings with interest, although she did not understand much of the hoopla. When the summer heat became too uncomfortable, Eleanor went back to Albany and took the children to Campobello. Franklin wired her there that Wilson had won the nomination.

In the fall of 1912, Franklin was up for reelection to the state senate, but he was in no shape to campaign. Both he and Eleanor were ill with typhoid fever, which they had contracted by drinking contaminated water on the boat ride back from Campobello. Franklin hired Louis Howe, a newspaper reporter from Albany, to run his campaign. Howe, who had early recognized great potential in both Franklin and Eleanor, agreed, and he won the election for Franklin. Moving back to their house in New York City, Eleanor and Franklin rented two rooms in a hotel in Albany. Franklin stayed in the hotel, while Eleanor went to Albany on Mondays and returned to New York on Thursdays to be with the children on the weekends.

They Move to Washington

On March 4, 1913, Eleanor and Franklin went to Washington to attend Wilson's inauguration. Wilson rewarded Franklin for his help at the convention by appointing him assistant secretary of the navy. Franklin accepted, resigned from the state senate in New York, and moved to Washington with Eleanor and the children.

Eleanor would be twenty-nine in October; Franklin had turned thirty-one in January. They already had some friends in Washington and quickly made more. Soon they were going out or entertaining almost every evening; in addition, Eleanor made courtesy calls in the afternoons to wives of other government officials. To help with the correspondence and scheduling, Eleanor hired a social secretary,

Politics and Public Service

When Franklin won a seat in the state legislature, both he and Eleanor entered public service. She tells of the change in Autobiography.

"Here in Albany began for the first time a dual existence for me, which was to last all the rest of my life. Public service, whether my husband was in or out of office, was to be a part of our daily life from now on. To him it was a career in which he was completely absorbed. He probably could not have formulated his political philosophy at that time as he could later, but the science of government was interesting—and people, the ability to understand them, the play of his own personality on theirs, was a fascinating study to him.

I still lived under the compulsion of my early training; duty was perhaps the motivating force of my life, often excluding what might have been joy or pleasure. I looked at everything from the point of view of what I ought to do, rarely from the standpoint of what I wanted to do. There were times when I almost forgot that there was such a thing as wanting anything. So I took an interest in politics. It was a wife's duty to be interested in whatever interested her husband, whether it was politics, books, or a particular dish for dinner."

Lucy Mercer, who soon became a family friend as well.

Franklin became busier and busier in his new job, especially in late 1916 and early 1917. The United States was being drawn into World War I, despite President Wilson's efforts to avoid that drastic step. On April 16, 1917, the United States declared war against Germany. Eleanor helped organize the Navy Red Cross and distributed free wool for knitting scarves, gloves, and the like for the armed forces. She joined the Red Cross canteen, where servicemen came for coffee, soup, sandwiches, and conversation. Working two or three shifts a week, Eleanor did whatever needed doing—making sandwiches, serving food, mopping floors.

Taking flowers and cigarettes, Eleanor visited the naval hospital every week. She talked with the wounded men and tried to cheer them. She went into wards for shell-shock victims, the men who could not bear the strains of war. When she noticed how understaffed the hospital was, she took action: "I could hardly wait to reach Secretary Lane [Department of the Interior] to tell him that I thought an investigation was in order and that he had better go see for himself."[30] He took her advice

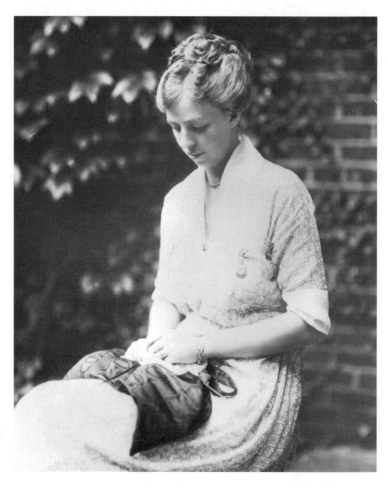

When the United States joined World War I, Eleanor helped organize Red Cross programs and regularly visited the naval hospital to comfort the wounded.

and got Congress to appropriate more funds for the hospital.

Still not satisfied, Eleanor persuaded the Red Cross to build a recreation room for "our men." Then she talked the Colonial Dames, a charitable organization, into giving five hundred dollars to open an occupational therapy unit for the patients. In her spare time she knitted.

Eleanor Faces a Crisis

On July 9, 1918, Franklin was sent overseas to determine the needs of the American naval bases in Europe. While he was gone, Eleanor worked at the canteen, sometimes twelve to fifteen hours a day. In September she learned that Franklin was on his way home but that he had pneumonia and that she should be at the pier to transport him home.

Eleanor and her mother-in-law took him to Sara's house. Eleanor made sure that Franklin was resting comfortably; then she began to unpack his bags. As she was sorting his mail, a packet of letters fell out. She picked them up and immediately recognized the familiar handwriting of her secretary, Lucy Mercer. They were love letters.

As far as Eleanor was concerned, Franklin's affair with Mercer had ended their thirteen-year marriage. She told him that he could get a divorce. When Sara heard of the affair, she was for a rare time in her life furious with her son. She warned Franklin that if he divorced Eleanor, she would cut him off without a cent. Louis Howe, who had stayed on as Franklin's adviser, told him that the scandal of divorce would finish his career in politics.

Franklin Delano Roosevelt during his tenure as assistant secretary of the navy. The post meant a move to Washington for Eleanor and the children.

Franklin Roosevelt was a practical man. He wanted to stay in politics, but without income from his mother, he could not afford to campaign. And he knew that Howe was right about the effects of a scandal. Howe went back and forth between Franklin and Eleanor and finally persuaded them to reconcile. Eleanor demanded that they maintain separate bedrooms from then on.

Learning to Think for Herself

Eleanor finally cut the strings that bound her to Franklin's mother, according to this account in Autobiography.

"My mother-in-law was distressed because I was not always available. I had long since ceased to be dependent on my mother-in-law. I wrote fewer letters and asked fewer questions and gave fewer confidences.

I do not mean that I was the better for this, but I was thinking things out for myself and becoming an individual. Had I never done this, perhaps I might have been saved some difficult experiences, but I have never regretted even my mistakes. They all added to my understanding of other human beings, and I came out in the end a more tolerant, understanding and charitable person. It has made life and the study of people more interesting than it could have been if I had remained in the conventional pattern."

Franklin voluntarily promised never to see Mercer again. Gradually, with Howe's help, Eleanor and Franklin built a partnership that would serve them both well.

Although Eleanor never relented on the terms she had set if she and Franklin were to stay together, she was able to maintain a congenial relationship with him. They were genuinely fond of each other and respected each other's abilities. She continued to support him in his political career, even as she developed her own career as a writer and speaker. They did grow apart in their personal lives, especially when Franklin became engrossed in World War II, but in their public lives they were an affectionate, effective team.

The war and Franklin's affair with Mercer were marked with stress and pain for Eleanor. Except for a brief "did you hear" note to Sara when Mercer later married Winthrop Rutherford, a wealthy widower with five children, Eleanor did not mention Mercer again. Eventually Eleanor emerged from this unhappy period with an expanded vision:

Out of these contacts with human beings during the war I became a more tolerant person, far less sure of my own beliefs and methods of action but more determined to try for certain ultimate objectives. I had gained some assurance about my ability to run things and the knowledge that there is joy in accomplishing a good job. I knew more about the human heart.[31]

Chapter

3 Independence at Last

I take things as they come.
— Eleanor Roosevelt

Franklin recuperated slowly from the pneumonia and did not report to Washington until the middle of October. Then on November 11, 1918, the armistice was signed, and the war ended. Franklin was ordered to go to Europe to close the naval operations there. He took Eleanor with him as a gesture of reconciliation.

After Franklin had finished his assignment, he and Eleanor went to France, where they toured some of the battlefields. Eleanor later described what they had seen: "We drove along the straight military roads with churned mud on either side of us, and deep shell holes here and there. Along the road there were occasional piles of stones with a stick stuck into them bearing the name of some vanished village."[32] Although Eleanor dreaded the next visit, she went to the Val de Grace, the military hospital where war veterans were undergoing multiple operations to restore their mutilated faces. Difficult as the experience was, she thought that she owed these veterans a visit.

When they returned to Washington, both tried hard to make their changed relationship work, although Eleanor suffered occasional periods of depression.

Then, as she had all of her life, she would retreat into one of her "Griselda moods," as she called them:

> One of my most maddening habits, which must infuriate all those who know me, is the habit, when my feelings are hurt or when I am annoyed, of simply shutting up like a clam, not telling anyone what is the matter, and being much too obviously humble and meek, feeling like a martyr and acting like one.[33]

As Eleanor developed confidence and independence, she gradually learned to control these episodes of self-pity.

Strengthened by Serenity

Eleanor's other escape was to drive to a cemetery in Washington's Rock Creek Park, where she would sit before a life-size bronze statue of a grieving woman. The sculpture was her late friend Henry Adams's memorial to his wife, who had committed suicide because she had heard rumors that he had been unfaithful. Eleanor confided years later to her friend Lorena Hickok that she had visited the statue during many troubled times.

Eleanor and FDR look peacefully at home in this photo, although by this time their marriage was strained.

Geoffrey Ward, in *A First-Class Temperament*, speculated that Eleanor "felt a sense of kinship with the long-dead woman who had believed herself betrayed, but she may also have permitted herself some pride that she had not succumbed to despair."[34] After studying the statue for half an hour or so, Eleanor would leave feeling strengthened by serenity.

Later, biographer Joseph Lash would recognize that Eleanor overcame tragedy with insight and courage:

> The personal disasters she had surmounted had taught her that although moments of stress and danger

could paralyze and destroy, they could also liberate and strengthen. She had turned her father's death into a constructive influence in her life. And instead of crushing her, the Lucy Mercer crisis had become [an] occasion of personal transcendence and growth.[35]

Eleanor Begins to Assert Herself

In 1919, renewing her resolve to become her own person, Eleanor began to move into an active life again and resumed some of her volunteer work. Visiting the wounded and the shell-shock veterans at St. Elizabeth's Hospital was her main project. She also dutifully made the expected social calls on other government wives, and she and Franklin entertained with dinner parties. She even began to stand up to Franklin's mother, despite Sara's vehement objections.

Money, food, social life, the children—Eleanor and Sara disagreed on almost every subject. Eleanor was tired of living in houses bought, furnished, and staffed by Sara. Eleanor dismissed Sara-appointed household servants (who answered to Sara, not Eleanor) and chose her own staff, whom she retained for years.

In 1920 Eleanor became active in an unexpected way. Franklin went to the Democratic National Convention in San Francisco in June while she took the children to Campobello. She soon received a wire saying that the delegates had chosen Franklin to be the vice-presidential candidate. Since women would be allowed to vote for the first time in the 1920 national election, Franklin took Eleanor on the campaign trail with him to attract women voters.

On the cross-country train tour, Eleanor learned to get along with the newspaper reporters. The biggest bonus for her, however, was getting to know Louis Howe, who was still Franklin's political adviser. She had never liked Howe, but

FDR, Eleanor, and Louis Howe (far left) on the campaign trail in 1920, the first year that women would be allowed to vote in a national election.

Making Money to Give Away

In Autobiography, *Eleanor explains why she needed to earn money to finance her projects.*

"In spite of my mother-in-law's dejection about my earning money, I think she eventually became reconciled to it, realizing that it enabled me to do many things for which my own income was insufficient and which would have been too great a financial drain on my husband. The money I had inherited from my parents' estate shrank during the depression years, and I ended with a very small yearly income. However, long before leaving New York City in 1933, I had begun to earn money through teaching, writing and radio work. I can remember my pleasure when I first was able to give some substantial help to the Women's Trade Union League in paying off the mortgage on their clubhouse.

With the first money I earned through commercial radio work, during the bad days of the depression, I established two places where girls who were unemployed and searching for work could have lunch and a place to rest. One was in the Women's Trade League clubhouse and the other was in the Girls' Service League headquarters on Madison Avenue. We gave the girls a hot lunch and snacks during the day, and provided facilities for sewing, mending, and the like."

he decided to change that situation. He had sensed her loneliness and her wish to participate rather than just look on. "Louis Howe began to break down my antagonism by knocking at my stateroom door and asking if he might discuss a speech with me. I was flattered and before long I found myself discussing a wide range of subjects."[36]

Not having really expected to win the election, Franklin had made plans to form a new law partnership in New York City. When he was defeated in November,

the Roosevelts moved back to New York, but Eleanor was not going back to her previous way of life. "I did not look forward to a winter of four days a week in New York with nothing but teas and luncheons and dinners to take up my time. The war had made that scene an impossible mode of living, so I mapped out a schedule for myself."[37]

Eleanor had taken only a few steps toward her resolved independence— enrolling in typing and shorthand classes and learning to cook—when she had to put her plans on hold while the family vacationed at Campobello in August 1921. After swimming in the nearby Bay of Fundy one afternoon, Franklin complained of being chilly and tired. As his temperature rose, his legs became painful and weak. When his condition continued to worsen, Eleanor sent for a specialist, who diagnosed polio. Franklin's legs would be permanently paralyzed. Sara then saw a chance to reclaim her son. She wanted him to retire to her Hyde Park mansion and live out his life as an invalid. Eleanor firmly resisted this plan and with Howe's help, she won.

Franklin learned to use crutches, but despite his zealous efforts, he never walked again. Leaning on crutches or someone's arm, he could swing his legs forward and appear to be walking, but he could not actually move on his own. Except for his paralyzed legs, however, he was again healthy. Howe persuaded Eleanor to take Franklin's place at political affairs during his convalescence so that he could stay active in politics, even if only second-handedly. Always speaking earnestly in her high-pitched voice, she gave more and more speeches to women's clubs and to political organizations. As biographer Joseph Lash pointed out, "His [Franklin's] survival as a public man [was] dependent on her resolution, her encouragement, her readiness to serve as

FDR's home on Campobello Island. While vacationing and swimming here in 1921, Roosevelt contracted polio.

his proxy in politics. He had always needed her, more than she was ever able to recognize or than he could usually bring himself to say."[38]

Eleanor Makes New Friends

Eleanor's substituting for Franklin at public affairs did keep him in the public eyes, but it also let her resume her efforts to become independent. Equally important, she had the chance to meet new people and to make some friends of her own. Earlier she had joined the League of Women

Eleanor with Esther Lape. Lape, along with Elizabeth Read, would become Eleanor's lifelong friend.

Voters. When she was put in charge of reporting national legislation to the New York members, she was aided by Elizabeth Read, a lawyer who helped Eleanor understand the legislation.

Meeting Read was a milestone in Eleanor's struggle to be her own person. Read and her apartment mate, Esther Lape, became the first adult friends who would help Eleanor become an individual in her own right. Eleanor recalled:

> I remember many pleasant evenings spent with Elizabeth and Esther in their little apartment. Their standards of work and their interests played a great part in what might be called "the intensive education of Eleanor Roosevelt" during the next few years.[39]

Eleanor's willingness to work and her commonsense approach brought her other lifelong friends—Rose Schneiderman of the Women's Trade Union League, Marion Dickerman and Nancy Cook of the Democratic Party, and reporter Lorena Hickok. These women helped Eleanor to discover her talents for leadership, organization, judgment, and perception while giving her the attention and affection that she craved. Eleanor was an able student and developed the talents she had never known she had; she quickly rose to leadership in almost every organization she joined.

Teaching

Marion Dickerman even opened a door into a profession that Eleanor had long wanted to enter—teaching. Aware of Eleanor's interest in young people, Dicker-

teaching methods on those of Mlle. Souvestre, Eleanor quickly became a stimulating teacher.

Eleanor Becomes First Lady of New York

Just as Eleanor was getting comfortable with her newly active life, she had to curb her independence again. Franklin had decided to reenter politics. Running for governor of New York in 1928, he narrowly won the election. Eleanor was happy for Franklin but sad for herself. Later she would write, "I sometimes wonder whether I really wanted Franklin to run."[40] Eleanor once again became a politician's wife, a position that she would fill from her sense of duty, not her preference. She reluctantly resigned from the Women's Division of the Democratic State Committee. She continued to teach at Todhunter, although the job meant commuting to New York every Sunday evening and returning to Albany on Wednesday afternoons. For the first time in her life, she was immensely successful; Eleanor wanted to teach as long as she could, even as the governor's wife.

Only Eleanor and Franklin moved into the governor's mansion. Anna was married; James was at Harvard; Elliott, Franklin Jr., and John were all attending Groton, a private boys' school—their father's alma mater—in Massachusetts. Enrolling her youngest son at Groton had been a milestone for Eleanor as well as for John. Sara remained at Hyde Park.

Eleanor quietly resumed her role as Franklin's assistant. They developed a system that would help them in later years in

Eleanor and sons return from a trip abroad in 1929. Pictured here are (from left to right) Eleanor, John, Marion Dickerman, FDR Jr., and Nancy Cook.

man, vice principal and later principal of Todhunter School, invited Eleanor to teach part-time at the Manhattan private girls' school. Beginning in 1927, Eleanor taught English, American literature, and American history to the sixteen- and seventeen-year olds. She later incorporated a course in current events into the curriculum and often took the girls on field trips to New York City. She took them to the New York courts, and when their parents would permit, into the slum areas. Modeling her

A Strong Sense of Personal Responsibility

In Life Is Meant to Be Lived *Joseph Lash includes Eleanor's definition of personal responsibility.*

"'Somewhere along the line of development,' Eleanor later wrote, 'we discover what we really are & then we make our real decision for which we are responsible. Make that decision primarily for yourself because you can never really live anyone else's life. The influence you exert is through your own life and what you become yourself.' The traits that were always there—above all, helpfulness, which is a form of love—now had a wider focus.

A period of intensive education in new realities began for Eleanor Roosevelt. It coincided with America's posing major challenges to American women. She would be a major participant in shaping the answers."

Washington. When Franklin wanted to inspect some state institution, such as a prison or a mental hospital, the superintendent of the facility would drive Franklin around the outside of the institution while Eleanor would inspect the inside. This system saved Franklin from the embarrassing necessity of being lifted in and out of cars in front of people. Eleanor quickly learned what kinds of information he wanted:

> At first my reports were highly unsatisfactory to him. I would tell him what was on the menu for the day and he would ask, "Did you look to see whether the inmates actually were getting that food?" I learned to look into the pots on the stove and to find out if the contents corresponded to the menu; I learned to notice whether the beds were too close together, and whether they were folded up and put

in closets or behind doors during the day, which would indicate that they filled the corridors at night; I learned to watch the patients' attitude towards the staff; and before the end of our years in Albany, I had become a fairly expert reporter on state institutions.[41]

As the governor's wife, Eleanor spent more and more time making speeches. Louis Howe helped her to improve her delivery. Through his efforts, Eleanor overcame a nervous giggle, and she managed to relax enough to lower her high-pitched voice a little. With her talent for using the language expressively, Eleanor became a popular speaker. As she became more knowledgeable about her subjects, she found that she could speak without notes, a talent that enhanced her authority as a speaker. By the time Franklin won a second term as governor, Eleanor had more speaking engagements than he had.

Franklin's reelection for a second term as governor of New York was so assured that it needed little attention from anyone, even Howe. After the Great Depression hit in 1929, Franklin initiated some new programs to put people back to work in New York that had attracted national attention. Eleanor wrote later:

[Franklin's running for a second term] was a very easy campaign, and I think it was a satisfaction to all of Franklin's supporters. This circumstance had the double advantage of making Franklin strong in the state and strong as a potential candidate for the presidency. That prospect did not interest me particularly but it did interest his supporters.[42]

Franklin Runs for President

In 1932 the Democratic National Convention was held in Chicago. Some of the children went with Franklin, but Eleanor

Sara, Eleanor, and Franklin Roosevelt during the years that Franklin would gain political prominence and seek the presidential nomination.

stayed in Albany. The reluctance that she had felt at his becoming governor intensified at the notion of his being nominated for the presidency:

From the personal standpoint, I did not want my husband to be president. I realized, however, that it was impossible to keep a man out of public service when that was what he wanted and was undoubtedly well equipped for. It was pure selfishness on my part, and I never mentioned my feelings on the subject to him. I did not work directly in the campaign, because I felt that was something done better by others, but I went on many of the trips and always did anything that Franklin thought would be helpful.[43]

He won the nomination and the subsequent election of November 1932. Like it or not, Eleanor was to be the first lady of the land. She did not like it, as she con-

Trying to Help Young People

Eleanor had been trying to find some way to help young people during the depression. Then she was asked to do just that, as she explains in This I Remember.

"One of the ideas I agreed to present to Franklin was that of setting up a national youth administration. Harry Hopkins [Franklin's assistant] and Aubrey Williams, Harry's deputy, knew how deeply troubled I had been from the beginning about the plight of the country's young people. One day they said, 'We have come to you about this because we do not feel we should talk to the President about it as yet. There may be bad political repercussions. We do not know that the country will accept it.'

I agreed to try to find out what Franklin's feelings were and to put before him their opinions and fears. I waited until my usual time for discussing questions with him and went into his room just before he went to sleep. I described the whole idea. He looked at me and asked: 'Do they think it is right to do this?' I said they thought it might be a great help to the young people, but it might be unwise politically. Then Franklin said: 'If it is the right thing to do for the young people, then it should be done.'

Shortly after, the NYA [National Youth Administration] came into being and undoubtedly benefited many young people."

fided to reporter Lorena Hickok, who would become one of her close friends. "I never wanted to be a President's wife, and I don't want it now." Knowing that her statement would be read all over the country, she added, "For him, of course, I'm glad—seriously. I am a Democrat, too. Now I shall have to work out my own salvation. I'm afraid it may be a little difficult. I know what Washington is like. I've lived there."[44] Eleanor's reluctance to be a president's wife echoed her objection to becoming the governor's wife: She did not want to be eclipsed and lose her independence and individuality.

Eleanor had long ago decided that if one confronted a problem or a situation openly and honestly, one could come to terms with it. By age forty-eight she had become skilled at confronting, changing, and adapting. That formula would help her to become a great and a unique first lady.

Between the time of Franklin's election and his inauguration, Eleanor served notice that not only would a new president move into the White House but a new first lady as well. Joseph Lash describes her first visit:

> When she had come down to Washington to look over the White House, she declined to be accompanied by a military aide or to be driven there in a government limousine. Instead she walked alone from the hotel.

> At the White House she briskly informed the chief usher of what she and Franklin wanted during the first days of their occupancy and "rattled it off as if she had known it her whole life," the admiring man said.[45]

After Franklin's inauguration, Eleanor was vocal about using her position as first lady to be influential in her own right.

Back in New York City the Women's Trade Union League honored her with a farewell dinner. She explained her intentions as first lady:

> I truly believe I understand what faces the great masses of people in the country today. I have no illusions that anyone can change the world in a short time. Things cannot be completely changed in five minutes. Yet I do believe that even a few people, who want to understand, to help and do the right thing for the great number of people instead of the few can help.[46]

4 First Lady by Election, Not Choice

I never wanted to be a president's wife.
—Eleanor Roosevelt

After Franklin's election, Eleanor told reporter Lorena Hickok, "There is just going to be plain, ordinary Mrs. Roosevelt. And that's all."[47] To prove her intentions, Eleanor made some changes in the White House and in the attentions usually shown first ladies. "Unconsciously I did many things that shocked the [White House] officials. My first act was to insist on running the elevator myself without waiting for one of the doormen to run it for me. That just wasn't done by the president's wife."[48]

"In order to hurry things along, I helped with the moving and placing of the furniture, much to the horror of the household staff."[49] Later she refused to be accompanied by Secret Service agents whenever she left the White House. Then she bought a light blue convertible with a rumble seat, and she declared that she would drive herself without a chauffeur or a police escort. When the head of Secret Service heard that decision, he insisted that she carry a gun in her car. She complied and even learned how to shoot it, but she never had the occasion to do so.

On March 6, 1933, two days after Franklin's inauguration, Eleanor announced her next change: She would hold a press conference that day and regularly thereafter. Few first ladies had given even an interview, and none had ever held a press conference. Furthermore, hoping to persuade editors to hire more women reporters, she invited only newspaperwomen. She was a little nervous at her first press conference, but Eleanor quickly became adept at fielding questions. She listened intently and answered each question directly, with no hedging. If any reporter asked a question that Eleanor considered private, she would courteously answer that the subject was personal and go on to the next question.

Arousing Controversy and Discussion

The collected transcripts of Eleanor's press conferences include her opinion of some national problems, descriptions of official functions, her concerns for young people, and revelations about herself, such as her ability to work long hours without rest. She spoke for herself, not for her husband's administration:

TOPIC:[Bill to allow immigration of] refugee children.

Eleanor kneels among women of the press corps during a conference in 1933. By inviting only female press members, Eleanor hoped to encourage the hiring of more women.

Mrs. Roosevelt: It is a matter of legislation, so until it is decided, I should make no official comment. I did, however, go on a committee in New York for arranging for the care of the children if they were allowed to enter. So you can draw your own conclusion.[50]

The relationship between Eleanor and the women's press corps was friendly but businesslike. The women believed that they had a right to ask her any question that would interest their readers. She asked for no favors, because she was—genially and cordially—in charge of the conference, as Joseph Lash illustrates:

"Sometimes I say things," she said to her press conference, "which I thoroughly understand are likely to cause unfavorable comment in some quarters, and perhaps you newspaper women think I should keep them off the record. What you don't understand is that perhaps I am making these statements on purpose to arouse controversy and thereby get the topics talked about and so get people to thinking about them."[51]

Eleanor sometimes made the front page of the newspaper without the aid of the women's press corps. In 1932, in the last months of President Hoover's administration, unemployed war veterans descended upon Washington to press Hoover to pay their promised bonuses immediately. Hoover's answer was to order General Douglas MacArthur to send the army to scatter them with tear gas and to destroy their campsite. Several people were injured.

Saving the Rabbit

In This I Remember *Eleanor tells about her visit to the home of a miner during one of her inspection trips for Franklin.*

"One story which I brought home from that trip I recounted at the dinner table one night. In a company house I visited, where the people had evidently seen better days, the man showed me his weekly pay slips. A small amount had been deducted toward his bill at the company store and for his rent and for oil for his mine lamp. These deductions left him less than a dollar in cash each week. There were six children in the family, and they acted as though they were afraid of strangers. I noticed a bowl on the table filled with scraps, the kind you or I might give to a dog, and I saw the children, evidently looking for their noonday meal, take a handful out of that bowl and go out munching. That was all they had to eat.

As I went out, two of the children had gathered enough courage to stand by the door, the little boy holding a white rabbit in his arms. It was evident that it was a most cherished pet. The little girl was thin and scrawny, and had a gleam in her eyes as she looked at her brother. She said, 'He thinks we are not going to eat it, but we are,' and at that the small boy fled down the road clutching the rabbit closer than ever.

It happened that William C. Bullitt [U.S. ambassador to France] was at dinner that night and I have always been grateful to him for the check he sent me the next day, saying he hoped it might help to keep the rabbit alive."

Eleanor's story about a struggling mining family compelled William C. Bullitt to assist the family financially.

In 1933, veterans came to confront President Roosevelt, who permitted them to stay in an old army camp, where they received food and medical care. He let them meet in a government auditorium where they talked with members of Congress. One afternoon Louis Howe suggested that Eleanor drive him by the veterans' camp. Then he persuaded her to stop to visit the veterans. While he napped in the car, she approached a line of veterans waiting for food:

> After their bowls were filled with food, I followed them into the big eating hall. I was invited to say a few words to them and then they sang for me some of the old Army songs.
>
> Then I got into the car and drove away. Everyone waved and I called "Good luck," and they answered, "Good-by and good luck to you."[52]

As Eleanor left, one man said, "Hoover sent the army. Roosevelt sent his wife."[53] When Franklin promised the men jobs in the Civilian Conservation Corps, they went home.

Eleanor continued to aid Franklin in other troubled situations as she had when he was governor. One of the first women to travel often by commercial airplane, she inspected federal prisons, the effects of the drought in the Midwest, and unemployment in the West Virginia coal mines. When she returned from such a trip, she and Franklin usually had an uninterrupted dinner so that she could give him a detailed report and answer all of his many questions. If they could not arrange a private dinner, she would leave her report and recommendations in a basket—the "Eleanor basket"—that sat on the floor

Eleanor was a great help to Franklin, often traveling across the country to report on economic conditions for the president.

near his bedside table. Franklin never told Eleanor whether she was doing a good job reporting, but he would sometimes pass her information on to his cabinet: "My missus says the people are leaving the Dust Bowl in droves because they haven't any chance there."[54]

On her inspection trips, Eleanor saw every possible aspect of the site and its problems. In the coal mines of Ohio, she put on a hard hat and went down two and a half miles into a mine to watch the miners work. The *New Yorker* magazine printed a cartoon that pictured two miners looking up from their shovels and saying, "For gosh sakes, here comes Mrs. Roosevelt!"[55]

Eleanor did not settle for seeing and talking with people just at their jobs; she also went into their homes and talked with their families. When she spoke with an individual, she gave that person her total

Inspecting Terrible Conditions

Eleanor's inspection trips became as important to her as they were to Franklin, because they gave her new reasons to take action, as shown by Doris Kearns Goodwin in No Ordinary Time.

"The following year [1934], Franklin had sent Eleanor to Puerto Rico to investigate reports that a great portion of the fancy embroidered linens that were coming into the United States from Puerto Rico were being made under terrible conditions. To the fury of the rich American colony in San Juan, Eleanor took reporters and photographers through muddy alleys and swamps to hundreds of foul-smelling hovels with no plumbing and no electricity, where women sat in the midst of filth embroidering cloth for minimal wages. Publicizing these findings, Eleanor called for American women to stop purchasing Puerto Rico's embroidered goods.

Later, Eleanor journeyed to the deep South and the 'Dustbowl.' Before long, her inspection trips had become as important to her as to her husband. 'I realized,' she said in a radio interview, 'that if I remained in the White House all the time I would lose touch with the rest of the world. I might have had a less crowded life, but I would begin to think that my life in Washington was representative of the rest of the country and that is a dangerous point of view.' So much did Eleanor travel, in fact, that the *Washington Star* once printed a humorous headline: 'Mrs. Roosevelt Spends Night at White House.' "

A cartoonist comically portrays the typical travel-filled day of Eleanor Roosevelt.

attention. Then she reported to Franklin what she had seen and heard. Through her efforts, Franklin Roosevelt was one of the best-informed presidents about social conditions across the country. Sometimes he would act on one of her recommendations, as when she insisted that the slums of Puerto Rico be replaced. The Puerto Ricans called their first housing project "Eleanor Roosevelt." Occasionally—even in her presence—Franklin would present Eleanor's idea as if it were his. Regardless of whether he gave her credit, people across the country believed that Eleanor and Franklin were interested in them and were trying to help them.

Eleanor Sponsors Arthurdale

Although Eleanor and Franklin led separate personal lives, they joined forces to form a powerful partnership with an urgent purpose: to improve the living conditions of the poverty-stricken victims of the Great Depression. While both had been trained in their youth to contribute to charities, only Eleanor had seen, talked with, and visited the needy in their homes. Franklin knew only what she had told him after her inspection tours. As William Youngs points out in his biography of Eleanor, "He heard about places like Scott's Run [a settlement of mining camps in West Virginia]; she came home with coal dust in her pores."[56]

Living conditions at Scott's Run, where the mines had been closed, were among the worst Eleanor had ever seen. Some families lived in tents. Children could go to school only when it was their turn to wear the single dress or pair of pants that the family shared. Everybody was hungry. Eleanor vowed to help.

Eleanor worked hard in an attempt to eliminate the terrible poverty she found in slums like this one in San Juan, Puerto Rico.

Children play in the Arthurdale housing development in West Virginia, where Eleanor proudly helped relocate depression victims. The development would cause a bit of a scandal for Eleanor.

Fortunately, earlier in 1933 Congress had allocated twenty-five million dollars to help depression victims get homestead loans. Franklin enthusiastically suggested that Eleanor plan to relocate some of the Scott's Run people to a new village that would attract industry and create new jobs for miners. She met with Louis Howe and Secretary of the Interior Harold Ickes; both men agreed to help her. "I'll buy the houses," said Howe. "Ickes, you buy the land. And Eleanor, you'll put the families in the houses."[57]

Everybody did his part, and fifty families from Scott's Run moved into the new development, which was named Arthurdale. Eleanor organized a school and paid part of the teachers' salaries with her own money. Proud of the project, Eleanor frequently brought people to see Arthurdale, where she soon knew several of the people by name.

Unfortunately, Howe had bought, over the phone and sight unseen, prefabricated houses built on Cape Cod for Arthurdale. Intended to be used as summer cottages on Cape Cod, the houses could not withstand the West Virginia winters without expensive modification. In addition, the water supply was not adequate. Congress attacked the idea of a planned community as socialism and refused to allocate any money to relocate a government industry there. Nor did any independent industry volunteer to move to Arthurdale. Eventually the people could not pay their rent and had to move.

Eleanor finally conceded that Arthurdale had not solved as many problems as Franklin and she had hoped. However, she did not consider the project a complete failure, as William Youngs describes:

> She knew another side to the experiment at Arthurdale. One woman's experience told the whole story; she was a homesteader whom Eleanor visited shortly before Christmas 1934. She was living in an attractive house with a cellar full of canned goods. Last Christmas, she told Eleanor, she had been in a hovel with two rooms and no windows. Christmas dinner had consisted of carrots. She had not even told the children it was Christmas. "This year," she said, "the children will each have a toy and we have a chicken, one of our own, that we are going to eat. It will be wonderful."[58]

She Exhausted Everyone Except Herself

To make her inspection trips and to develop her projects, Eleanor, who required minimal rest, worked herself and her secretaries long hours. Rising at 7:30 each

Eleanor, at her desk at the White House, meets with personal secretary Malvina Thompson and social secretary Edith P. Helm in 1941.

morning, she usually retired between midnight and 3:00 A.M. During those long hours, she routinely exercised or rode her horse after breakfast; talked briefly with Franklin; and discussed the day's activities with the chief usher, the housekeeper, and her social secretary, Edith Helm. Then she met with her personal secretary, Malvina (Tommy) Thompson, to discuss the day's mail, which Tommy would already have separated. Eleanor dictated answers to some letters, wrote some replies herself, and directed that the rest be forwarded to the person who could answer the writer's request—the secretary of labor, for example. Every letter got an answer from someone. Eleanor received more than 300,000 letters—most of them asking for some kind of help—her first year in the White House. She would also receive and make phone calls, entertain any dignitaries visiting Franklin, write articles for the newspapers and for her column in the *Ladies Home Companion*, and attend receptions. She once shook hands with thirty-one hundred members of the Daughters of the American Revolution in one hour.

Some Changes She Did Not Make

Two things Eleanor did not change after she became first lady were her attitudes toward food and relaxation. Food did not matter to her. As long as the food was wholesome, she would eat whatever was placed in front of her. She always said that Franklin felt the same way. On the contrary, he relished interesting gourmet foods, but somehow he could never penetrate her misconception. Their cook, Mrs.

Nesbitt, knew that Eleanor did not mind having the same food often. After Franklin had been served oatmeal for breakfast for several weeks, he sent Mrs. Nesbitt an advertisement for several kinds of cereal. She continued to serve him oatmeal. Franklin could never bring himself to fire anyone, and since Eleanor admired Mrs. Nesbitt's thrift, she wouldn't fire her either. White House food was not distinguished during the Roosevelt residency, not even when the president and his wife were entertaining.

Different Attitudes Toward Relaxation

Eleanor and Franklin were also at odds over the use of off-duty time. When Franklin left the Oval Office at the end of a day, he was relaxed by the time he got to their living quarters in the White House. He enjoyed a cocktail and banter with friends and colleagues before dinner. After dinner, he liked to play poker with his cronies or work on his lifetime project, his stamp collection. Eleanor thought light conversation was a waste of time; she did not approve of drinking or gambling, even for a few cents, and she was not a stamp collector. After dinner she returned to her quarters and answered more letters, wrote more articles, planned more speeches.

Eleanor realized that she lacked some traits that Franklin needed. She knew that his secretary, Miss LeHand (Missy), who lived on the third floor of the White House, enjoyed the same pastimes he did, even playing poker. Eleanor was willing to let Missy substitute for her. Some people called Missy Franklin's "other wife." If Eleanor heard the gossip, she did not acknowledge it. She maintained cordial relations with Missy.

Eleanor Writes Her First Book

Somehow in all of those work-filled hours of her first year as first lady, Eleanor found time to write a book, *It's Up to the Women*, published in 1933. The main theme of her book was that women must play a major role in leading the nation to recovery from the Great Depression. In one of her earliest feminist statements, she wrote in the foreword:

> There have been other great crises in our country and I think if we read our history carefully, we will find that the success of our nation in meeting them was very largely due to the women in those trying times. Upon them fell a far heavier burden and responsibility than any of us realize.[59]

After counseling women about time management, family health, and house-

FDR, Eleanor, and Missy LeHand (center) swim in Hyde Park in 1930. Some people called Missy "Franklin's other wife."

Life on the Lecture Circuit

Whether she liked it or not, Eleanor was closely guarded on her lecture tours. She describes two humorous incidents involving her security in This I Remember.

"Because I was under contract for the lecture trips, I had to keep to my schedule. That meant work and discipline—and I felt I needed both. In addition, I really did enjoy getting away to less formal surroundings, though I was to find that going on lecture trips did not always mean that I succeeded in being 'unofficial.' On occasion, I was more guarded and watched over than in Washington. Late one night in Detroit when we opened the door of our suite in the hotel to go out and drop some letters in the mail chute, three men rushed out of the adjoining room and asked what was wrong. We discovered that they were plain-clothes men assigned to watch over me.

In another city, Little Rock, Arkansas, the mayor assigned two big, husky motor-cycle policemen to escort me during the day. In the morning I decided to have a shampoo, so I made an appointment at a hair-dressing shop. I was escorted by the policemen, but fully expected they would leave me at the door. To my surprise they came right into the shop with me and sat where they could watch the whole operation, much to the amusement and perhaps annoyance of the other customers."

hold economy, Eleanor discussed women's issues relating to jobs, voting, working conditions, and business training. She concluded with this declaration:

I am merely pointing out that women have always been a tremendous power in the destiny of the world and with so many of them now holding important positions and receiving recognition and earning the respect of the men as well as the members of their own sex, it seems more than ever that in this crisis, *It's Up to the Women!*[60]

Although some critics condemned Eleanor's writing—in newspaper and magazine articles, as well as in her book—as wordy and trivial, women of the country quickly became enthusiastic readers. They liked her unpretentious, conversational style and her concerns with their problems. By the end of the Roosevelts' first year in the White House, Eleanor was as popular as Franklin.

5 The Roosevelt Team

I'm the agitator; he's the politician.
—Eleanor Roosevelt

Although both Eleanor and Franklin wanted to improve the lives of the American people, Franklin was a politician first and a reformer second. He had to balance his personal opinions against the loss of support of Congress that might result from his position. He would not endorse a proposed bill, even if he believed in it, if

Frances Perkins became labor commissioner under FDR due to Eleanor's urging. Eleanor often suggested women for posts, hoping to promote women's rights.

doing so would antagonize a bloc of congressmen whose support he needed for another bill or for the next election. He could support the proposal indirectly, however, by letting Eleanor speak about it.

"'Do you mind if I say what I think?' Eleanor once asked her husband.

'No, certainly not,' he replied. 'You can say anything you want. I can always say, Well, that is my wife; I can't do anything about her.'"[61]

Eleanor did not worry about the political fallout that her own opinions would cause. She used her position as first lady to expose and remedy social problems, especially in identifying the rights of women and minorities, recognizing youth and their anxieties, reducing poverty, and establishing peace.

Eleanor Urges Equal Rights for Women

Eleanor had been working for women's rights since Franklin was governor when she suggested he appoint women to government positions. While he was making his staff appointments during a working vacation at Warm Springs, Georgia, she wrote, "I hope you will consider making

Frances Perkins Labor Commissioner."[62] He did, and later, as president, he named her to his cabinet as secretary of labor, the first woman to be appointed to a presidential cabinet.

Eleanor specified as early as 1933 that women should have certain rights: "Women should receive equal pay for equal work and they should also work the same hours and insist on the same good working conditions and the same rights of representation that men have."[63] These opinions did not endear her to the men's labor unions, which did not like the idea that women would be competing for men's jobs. Eleanor was not so naive as to think that women would receive no resistance as they were assimilated into the men's working world. In *It's Up to the Women,* she wrote, "During the next few years, at least, every woman in public office will be watched far more carefully than a man holding a similar position, and she will be acting as a pioneer preparing the way for many other women who will follow in her footsteps."[64] She urged women to apply not only for political appointments but also to investigate technical and research positions in the nonpolitical government services as well.

Symbols of New Thoughts and Ideas

On one occasion, someone asked Eleanor's opinion about whom she considered the three greatest women of all time. Her answer confirmed her conviction that women have the right to seek fulfillment according to their individual talents. She named nurse Florence Nightingale, scientist Marie Curie, and writer Harriet Beecher Stowe. Then she justified her choices:

> I have used these three women simply as symbols of the development of new phases in women's experience. I doubt if any human beings, just by themselves, are very important, but when they start a new trend of thought and action, they are apt to symbolize for their contemporaries and for the future a new idea, and therefore they become important.[65]

Eleanor Confronts Racial Prejudice

Identifying the rights of minorities was a real challenge for Eleanor because her Victorian upbringing had trained her to regard blacks as inferiors. However, working with some black leaders expanded and refocused her vision of the treatment of minorities. Walter White, head of the National Association for the Advancement of Colored People (NAACP), asked for and received her help in advocating national antilynching legislation. The legislation was necessary, because in some states, lynching continued to go unpunished. Blacks had been the victims of recorded and unrecorded lynchings for many years. Twenty-four blacks had been lynched in 1933, for example. Eleanor arranged for White to meet with Franklin. Although the president wholeheartedly supported an antilynching bill, he knew that to do so publicly would alienate not only the bloc of Southern Democrats but also some conservative Republicans. The antilynching bill did not pass.

Lynchings

The Reader's Companion to American History *includes a brief history of lynching in the United States.*

"Lynching is the practice whereby a mob—usually several dozen or several hundred persons—takes the law into its own hands in order to injure and kill a person accused of some wrongdoing. The alleged offense can range from a serious crime like theft or murder to a mere violation of local customs and sensibilities. The issue of the victim's guilt is usually secondary, since the mob serves as prosecutor, judge, jury, and executioner.

Between 1882 (when reliable statistics were first collected) and 1968 (when the classic forms of lynching had disappeared), 4,743 persons died of lynching, 3,446 of them black men and women. Although lynchings declined somewhat in the twentieth century, there were still 97 in 1908 (89 black, 8 white), 83 in the racially troubled postwar year of 1919 (76, 7, plus some 25 race riots), 30 in 1926 (23, 7), and 28 in 1933 (24, 4).

Statistics do not tell the entire story, however. These were *recorded* lynchings; others were never reported beyond the community involved."

Eleanor was disappointed but not discouraged. In 1936 she invited world-renown black contralto Marian Anderson to sing at the White House, an action that outraged many of Eleanor's critics and most segregationists. Undeterred, she approved of a public recital by Anderson in Washington in 1939. One problem immediately surfaced. The Daughters of the American Revolution (DAR), of which Eleanor had long been a proud member, refused to let Marian Anderson—or any other black—sing in Constitution Hall, which the group owned. After resigning from the DAR in protest, Eleanor worked with Secretary of the Interior Ickes, who looked kindly on the blacks, to stage a concert for Anderson on the steps of the Lincoln Memorial. On Easter Sunday afternoon, April 9, 1939, a crowd of seventy-five thousand stood shivering in the cold wind to hear the distinguished contralto sing. "When I sang that day," Marian Anderson wrote later, "I was singing to the entire nation."[66]

Taking a Stance

In 1938 Eleanor attended a meeting of the Southern Conference for Human Welfare in Birmingham, Alabama, with Mary McLeod Bethune, a famous black educator.

Eleanor presents the Springarn Medal of the NAACP to Marian Anderson in Richmond, Virginia, in 1939.

Born in the rural South, Mary McLeod Bethune had seen some of her sixteen brothers and sisters sold into slavery. Trained to be a missionary, she had moved to Washington to become director of Negro affairs for the National Youth Administration. Eleanor and Mrs. Bethune could not even sit together at the meeting because Birmingham's segregation law mandated that blacks and whites had to remain separate. The blacks sat on one side of the aisle; the whites sat on the other side. Eleanor sat with the black group. When a policeman insisted that she join the white group, she moved her chair into the middle of the aisle between the two groups. She sat there throughout the conference.

Eleanor continued to seize every opportunity to show her rejection of racial prejudice. Her critics were especially incensed by the friendly support she extended to the black participants. When Franklin's advisers suggested that he tell her that she was going too far and to withdraw a little, he refused.

A Fight Against Inequality

After becoming a member of the NAACP in 1939, Eleanor joined its leaders in asking the government to act decisively to ban discrimination in the armed forces and in defense work. The government responded reluctantly and made a few token changes, but the military camps were still segregated. When Eleanor learned that ten to twenty seats in the back row of camp theaters were reserved for blacks, that at the post exchanges blacks could not eat in the refreshment centers, that on camp buses blacks could sit only in the back of the bus, and that blacks were kept from active duty, she wrote Chief of Staff General George Marshall and insisted that he stop such unequal treatment. He ordered an investigation of her accusations and found that they were true. Finally, on March 10, 1943, the War Department sent out a new order to all camps: All "white" and "colored" signs were to be removed, and all recreational facilities were to be open to all service personnel. In April 1943 the first unit of black combat pilots left for overseas duty. They had been fully trained and waiting since September 1942.

In her book *No Ordinary Time*, Doris Goodwin praises Eleanor for improving economic opportunities for blacks in Franklin's New Deal programs:

Largely because of Eleanor Roosevelt, black complaints against New Deal economic programs received a hearing at the White House, and the president agreed to sign an executive order barring discrimination in the administration of WPA [Works Progress Administration] projects. From that point on, the Negroes' share in the New Deal expanded.[67]

With Eleanor's strong support, in 1944 Franklin also proposed a new bill of rights that would provide economic security for all American citizens—the rights to a job, livable earnings, adequate housing, medical care, and old age assistance. Eleanor talked about this proposal whenever she could. However, since only new taxes could support the program, Congress di-

Eleanor and educator Mary McLeod Bethune at the Second National Conference on Negro Youth. When the two could not sit together at a conference because of segregation, Eleanor sat on the black side with Mary.

luted the bill to a fraction of Franklin's request. Franklin vetoed the Congress version; Congress overruled his veto. The Roosevelts' second bill of rights—written as they wanted—was defeated.

She Could Be Misled

Eleanor attempted to support the rights of young people, too. In the 1930s she endorsed the American Youth Congress (AYC), which included members of three youth organizations: the Young Men's Christian Association, the American League for Peace, and the Popular Front. The AYC members were liberal idealists who believed in communism. People across the country severely criticized her for working with a communist-backed group. She defended her involvement with AYC, saying, "Gradually I began to work with them, for it seemed to me a good way to find out what was happening to young people and what they were thinking."[68] She attended their meetings, advised them, and gave them money.

Thinking that she could nudge them back to democratic beliefs, she spoke to the AYC on May 26, 1940. "You don't want to go to war. I don't want to go to war. But war may come to us." After noting that England had been unprepared for Hitler's onslaught, she added that it was "necessary to arm in order to avoid the same crisis."[69] When the delegates did not waver from their antiarmament isolationism, Eleanor severed her relationship with AYC.

Out of her work with these youth groups came a very important relationship. Despite the twenty-five year difference in their ages, Eleanor and American

Answering the Many Questions

"What do you think can and should be done to overcome the anti-Semitism in this country?

I think much can be done to overcome anti-Semitism in this country. Jewish people themselves can help by trying to be as natural and unselfconscious as possible. They can go about their own lives, doing the things they have always done, but trying not to be too aggressive or too ingratiating or flattering to the people who they suspect are sizing them up. On the other hand, all the rest of us can try to forget that the people with whom we associate belong to any particular race or to any particular religion. We can treat others with the respect due human beings and we will receive respect in return, regardless of race, color, or creed."

Student Union secretary Joseph Lash forged a friendship that nurtured both of them as long as Eleanor lived.

To the critics who pointed an accusing finger at her for associating with this group, she answered, "I have never said anywhere that I would rather see young people associated with communism. But I have said that I would rather see the young people actually at work, even if I considered that they were doing things that were a mistake."[70]

Eleanor Aids Refugees

In the middle of Franklin's second term, he turned his attention to international affairs. A storm was brewing as the dictator of Germany, Adolf Hitler, began his assault of Europe. Engrossed with conferring with leaders of the endangered countries, Franklin had to put domestic affairs aside for a while. Both Eleanor and Franklin were sure Hitler's next target would be England. Eleanor shifted some of her focus to a group of would-be victims of Hitler's aggression, England's children. People in both the United States and England wanted to evacuate the children.

In 1940, Eleanor pulled together the members of the American Friends Service Committee, the German-Jewish Children's Aide, and the Committee for Catholic Refugees to devise a way to help children in England elude the Nazis. With Eleanor as honorary chairwoman, the group formed the United States Committee for the Care of European Children. Headed by Chicago businessman Marshall Field, the new committee persuaded the U.S. Department of State to grant visitors' visas to the children, so that they could stay in the United States until the danger had passed; then they could return home. When the committee solicited American families to accept the children, thousands of families responded.

The plan did not include Jewish children who had fled Germany. (At first Hitler was content to drive Jews out of Germany; later he would send them to concentration camps.) Joe Lash brought two members of the European underground, Karl Frank and Joseph Buttinger, to Eleanor's apartment in New York City to ask for help in relocating Jewish refugees, both adults and children, who had been stranded in Spain, France, and Portugal. Agreeing to help, Eleanor imme-diately called Franklin, who emphatically refused. Although sympathetic to the children's plight, Franklin was afraid that Nazis would disguise themselves as refugees and spy on the United States.

Eleanor appealed to her friend Sumner Welles in the State Department, who eventually started an emergency program to help the refugees. Frank kept Eleanor informed: "I know it is due to your interest that hundreds of people had been granted visitors' visas."[71] Frank wrote Eleanor the day after the emergency program had been put into operation. Eventually over 100,000 refugees from Nazism were safely living in the United States.

In the spring of 1941, with the threat that the United States could become involved in the war at any time, the president

Businessman Marshall Field with the European refugee children he helped bring to New York in 1940.

Consideration for Young People

Stella Hershan, in A Woman of Quality, *describes an incident in which a fourteen-year-old high school reporter was sent to interview Eleanor at a press conference attended by television, radio, and newspaper reporters.*

"That morning at 10:30, a mass press interview was scheduled at the club upon Mrs. Roosevelt's arrival and my editor sent me to cover the event. Punctual to the minute, Eleanor Roosevelt smiled her way through the crowd.

Almost instantly, questions were fired at her hard and fast. I was quite dazed by the speed and, although I had prepared several questions, they seemed too trivial to ask. Once or twice I tried to open my mouth but there was always another reporter ahead of me. The interview was almost over and I had not had a chance to pose a single question.

Abruptly, quite without warning, Mrs. Roosevelt looked directly at me and the friend who had accompanied me.

'How about these young people?' she asked. 'They didn't have a chance to ask anything.'

Everyone looked our way. My own voice sounded small and high-pitched as I forced myself to pose a question. 'What kind of music,' I asked, 'do Russian teenagers like?' I thought I heard some snicker from the veteran reporters. Mrs. Roosevelt, however, gazed at me thoughtfully as she began to speak of Russian youths who, much as American young people, seemed to have preference for rock and roll."

created the Office of Civil Defense (OCD). Franklin appointed Mayor Fiorello La-Guardia of New York City to direct this countrywide organization of volunteers. When several months had passed and the mayor had done little, Eleanor criticized the lack of progress. LaGuardia then invited Eleanor to be assistant director. Despite having qualms about being criticized for taking a government job, she accepted. It was fall before she could report for work, assisted by her friend Elinor Morgenthau. Although the two organized and expanded the scope of the OCD, opponents of Franklin's programs criticized every step Eleanor took. She had never before received such wide criticism. Rather then undermine Franklin's work, Eleanor resigned. Even her supporters agreed that LaGuardia should not have offered her the job, she should not have accepted it, and Franklin should not have approved her taking it. Later she wrote in *This I Remember*, "I had done the best I could while I was there, but as long as I held a government position, even as a volunteer, I offered a way to get at the president and in war time it is not politically wise to attack the president."[72]

The United States Enters World War II

Then the day Eleanor and Franklin had prepared for came. The Japanese bombed Pearl Harbor on December 7, 1941, thereby drawing the United States into the war. Late that afternoon Franklin dictated his famous "a day which will live in infamy" speech to Grace Tully, his secretary. He would address Congress the next morning. In her suite, Eleanor was working on her weekly radio show. At 6:30 she told the American people, "For months now, the knowledge that something of this kind might happen has been hanging over our heads. Whatever is asked of us, I am sure we can accomplish it; we are the free and unconquerable people of the United States of America."[73]

Wanting to serve the war effort, Eleanor suggested that she accept an invitation from the king and queen of England to visit them. While in England, she would study the ways in which English women were bolstering their country during the war. With Franklin's approval, she flew to England in October 1942. Arriving in London, she was shocked and saddened by the extensive damage German bombs had wreaked. After a two-day courtesy visit with the royal family, Eleanor moved into an apartment and began a sched-

ule crowded with meetings, speeches, receptions, and inspections. Her pace left the British reporters chasing after her. They reported in the *London Daily Mail* that she walked "fifty miles through factories, clubs, and hospitals."[74] Eleanor observed British women being trained to substitute for men at various jobs, even repairing trucks.

She also reviewed American troops and talked with the men. Once her driver got lost when he was taking her to see her son Elliott, who was stationed in England. The driver called the embassy to ask for directions: "Rover [Eleanor's code name] has lost her pup [Elliott]."[75] When she finally started home, a British Office of War Information staff member said, "Mrs. Roosevelt has done more to bring a real understanding of the spirit of the United States to the people of Britain than any other single American who has ever visited these islands."[76]

Eleanor rides with Queen Elizabeth during her trip to England in 1942. More than a diplomatic visit, the trip helped Eleanor to study the ways English women were helping the war effort.

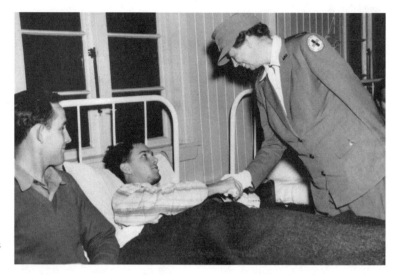

Eleanor speaks with a wounded soldier. Eleanor's trips to battlefield hospitals drew criticism from Franklin.

Since her trip to England had been so successful, Eleanor wanted to travel to Russia and China, or even to Detroit where race riots were erupting. Franklin would approve none of these requests, however, because the potential danger was too great. Even Detroit, where months of racial conflicts had finally exploded into violence, was too risky a place for Eleanor to visit. As Joseph Lash points out, "It was dangerous to permit a woman who refused to suppress the promptings of her conscience and imagination to visit the areas where the most searching test of the Christian ethic was taking shape."[77]

Eleanor Goes to the South Pacific

Franklin did agree to Eleanor's visiting American troops in the South Pacific war area, much to the dismay of Admiral William Halsey, chief of naval operations in the Pacific. He considered her a snoopy busybody.

Limited to forty-four pounds of luggage, which included her old portable typewriter (she continued to write "My Day" wherever she was), she took only Red Cross uniforms—the slate blue cap, skirt, jacket, and white blouse. The fifty-nine-year-old first lady traveled alone this time in an unheated four-engine army plane. After a rest stop in Hawaii, the crew flew her to Christmas Island.

Rising at reveille, as she did in every camp, Eleanor ate breakfast with the enlisted men. Then, escorted by two enlisted men as she had requested, she toured the base and visited the hospital. She went into every ward, stopped at every bed to talk with every patient, and took messages that she would deliver when she returned home.

She wrote Franklin a quick report: Older men should not be assigned to that hot climate for more than two years; the younger men could adjust better to the heat. White and colored men were working well together. They needed more recreation, especially phonographs and phonograph needles. Worries that the

MacArthur Versus Roosevelt

On her South Pacific tour, Eleanor wanted to visit New Guinea, but General Douglas MacArthur had no time for her. Joseph Lash describes Eleanor's reaction in Eleanor and Franklin.

"She wanted to go to New Guinea but, as she wrote sardonically to Doris Fleeson, 'General MacArthur was too busy to bother with a lady.' Her letter to Franklin was irate: 'Word came last night from Gen. MacArthur that it would require too many high-ranking officers to escort me to Port Moresby & he cld not spare them at this time when a push is on. This is the kind of thing that seems to me silly. I'd rather have a Sergeant & I'd see and hear more but I must have a General. The newspapers here complain that I see none of the plain people. Neither do I really see any of the plain soldiers. I have an MP [military police] escort everywhere that wld do you credit. I have all the pomp & restriction & none of the power! I'm coming home this time & go in a factory!'

General MacArthur would not be bothered with her, and the staff aide whom he detailed to escort her in Australia was anything but pleased when the assignment was first handed to him. However, like Admiral Halsey, the aide came away a changed man. In an article he later wrote for the *Christian Advocate* he said: 'When she chatted with the men she said things Mothers say, little things men never think of and couldn't put into words if they did. Her voice was like a mother's, too. Mrs. Roosevelt went through hospital wards by the hundreds. In each she made a point of stopping by each bed, shaking hands, and saying some nice, motherlike thing. Maybe it sounds funny, but she left behind her many a tough battletorn GI blowing his nose and swearing at the cold he had recently picked up.' "

General Douglas MacArthur was frustrated and angry when Eleanor wanted to visit troops in New Guinea.

Eleanor is escorted by a private while looking at wrecked Japanese Zeros on her trip to Guadalcanal in 1943.

men might find her boring were unfounded, she was pleased to report, "but as far as I can tell my being here is giving them a kick."[78]

Eleanor especially wanted to go to Guadalcanal because Joe Lash was stationed there. When she landed in New Caledonia and gave Admiral Halsey Franklin's letter approving the trip—if Admiral Halsey agreed—he refused to grant her permission. "'Guadalcanal is no place for you, Ma'am!' Halsey brusquely responded. 'If you fly to Guadalcanal, I'll have to provide a fighter escort for you, and I haven't got one to spare.'"[79] Fortunately for Eleanor, her attention to the servicemen so impressed him that he finally let her go. Once there, she went to the cemetery where thousands of American servicemen were buried, toured several hospitals, had lunch with a general and dinner with Admiral Halsey, and still had time to talk with Joe Lash.

When Eleanor returned to the United States, she had traveled twenty-three thousand miles and had visited Australia, New Zealand, and seventeen South Pacific islands. Landing in Washington on September 25, 1943, she reported to the president all that she had seen and heard. Then, in a state of delayed shock, Eleanor became deeply depressed as she remembered the wounded servicemen and the rows of American graves. The futility of war engulfed her. On September 27 she described her trip during a radio broadcast that she ended with a solemn plea for racial and religious tolerance. The price of war was too great.

The war had taken its toll on Franklin as well as on Eleanor. His face was pale and lined with the stress of directing the U.S. part in a world war. Nonetheless he accepted the nomination and election for a fourth term as president. Soon after his fourth inaugural in January 1945,

War Threatens Their Partnership

Although Eleanor and Franklin's marriage had failed, their partnership as politicians and reformers was highly successful. Her alarm at his becoming so engrossed with foreign affairs was understandable, as Doris Kearns Goodwin explains in No Ordinary Time.

"During Franklin's years as governor and president, the Roosevelts became so deeply involved with one another that they seemed like two halves of a single whole whose lives, as New Deal economist Rexford Tugwell put it, 'were joined in a common cause.' Her astonishing travels, her strong convictions, her curiosity about almost every phase of the nation's life, from slum clearance to experimental beehives, from rural electrification to country dances, provided fascinating material for endless conversations, arguments, and debates.

Their working partnership involved the creation of a shared emotional territory in which they could relate to each other with abiding love and respect. To be sure, on some occasions, she irritated and even exasperated him, but he never ceased to respect and admire her. Nor did she ever stop loving him. 'I hated to see you go. . . ,' Eleanor wrote Franklin in the 1930s as he set out on a journey to Europe. 'We are really very dependent on each other though we do see so little of each other.'

Understanding the nature of their relationship, it is not surprising, then, that Eleanor anguished so much in the spring of 1940 over the fear that her partnership would break apart. The husband who had been her close friend would now be more remote, his attention directed to international concerns. The man who loved nothing more than the detailed stories of her travels, now had little time and less inclination to listen to her."

Though the Roosevelts sustained a successful working relationship, the demands of the presidency put a strain on their marriage.

Franklin Roosevelt remains the only president to be elected to four terms.

Franklin went to Yalta for a summit meeting with British prime minister Winston Churchill and Soviet premier Joseph Stalin. In April he went to Warm Springs for a working vacation with his cousins, Laura Delano and Margaret Suckley, whose company he enjoyed, and Grace Tully. On April 12 Eleanor held her regular press conference. Her main point that morning was a straightforward message: "A United Nations organization is for the very purpose of making it possible that all the world's opinions will have a clearing place."[80] She directed her statement at those who believed that the United States could make worldwide decisions without consulting other countries. Some members of Congress held that opinion, as did some other countries that wanted the United States to assume that responsibility. World War II had convinced Eleanor that only worldwide peace efforts could prevent World War III.

After her news conference, Eleanor hosted a luncheon for Nila Magidoff, a lecturer for Russian War Relief. At three o'clock, while she was talking with a U.S. adviser to the United Nations, her secretary called her to the telephone. Cousin Laura Delano had told her that Franklin had fainted and had been taken to his bed. After calling Franklin's physician, Dr. McIntire, Eleanor followed his advice and kept a four o'clock appointment to speak at a fund-raiser. She had just finished her speech when she was called to the telephone. "Steve Early, very much upset, asked me to come home at once. I did not even ask why. I knew in my heart something dreadful had happened."[81] When she reached her sitting room in the White House, Steve Early and Dr. McIntire came in to tell her that Franklin had died.

6 Private Citizen Again

I would be on my own.

—Eleanor Roosevelt

Eleanor's response to the news of Franklin's death was, "Though this was a terrible blow, somehow you had no choice to think of it as a personal sorrow. It was the sorrow of all those to whom this man who now lay dead, and who happened to be my husband, had been a symbol of strength and fortitude."[82] Then she sent for Vice President Harry Truman. While waiting for him, she called her four sons, who were all on active duty. Her daughter, Anna, was living in the White House at the time.

When Truman entered her sitting room at 5:30 P.M., Eleanor walked toward him.

> "Harry," she said quietly, "the President is dead."
>
> Stunned and momentarily speechless, he finally asked, "Is there anything I can do for you?"
>
> She reminded him gently, "Is there anything we can do for you? For you are the one in trouble now."[83]

At the moment of Franklin's death, Eleanor had ceased being first lady, an act that became official when Truman was sworn in as president at seven o'clock that evening. Then Truman considerately approved her flying to Warm Springs in a government plane, a privilege she herself could no longer claim.

After arriving at Warm Springs, Eleanor listened as first Grace Tully, then cousin Margaret described Franklin's collapse. When cousin Laura's turn came, she

Harry S. Truman became president when Franklin Roosevelt died in office.

Eleanor with her daughter, Anna. Although Eleanor was proud of her children, she spent little time rearing them and consequently was not close to them.

told Eleanor more devastating news; she brought out that Franklin had continued to see Lucy Mercer Rutherford through the years and that Rutherford and her artist friend had been in the guest house the last three days. The artist had been painting a portrait of Franklin. Laura also told Eleanor that Lucy had been a guest in the White House several times while Eleanor was away on trips and that Anna had been hostess at those dinners. Eleanor did not react outwardly to Laura's devastating news. She turned and walked into Franklin's bedroom where he lay, closed the door, and stayed about five minutes. When she emerged, she arranged to accompany his body back to Washington.

On the train, as Franklin lay in state in the lighted rear car, four honor guards

from the armed services stood at attention at the four corners of the casket. Eleanor remained in her darkened compartment: "I lay in my berth with the window shades up, looking out at the countryside he loved and watching the faces of the people at stations and even at crossroads, who came to pay their tribute all through the night."[84]

Franklin's state funeral was held in the East Room of the White House. Only Elliott could get a leave to join Anna and Eleanor. According to Franklin's wishes, he was buried in the rose garden at Hyde Park.

Although the Trumans had assured Eleanor that she could take all of the time she needed to vacate the White House, she told them that she would be out by Friday, April 20. Early on Monday, the sixteenth, she started packing. She paused long enough to take Bess and Margaret Truman, the president's wife and daughter, on a tour of the White House. They were appalled at the state of disrepair. Eleanor had been too busy to think about redecorating

FDR's funeral procession in Washington, D.C.

Leaving the White House

In On My Own, *the third volume of her autobiography, Eleanor describes her feelings as she leaves the White House as Eleanor Roosevelt, former first lady.*

"I rode down in the old cagelike White House elevator that April morning of 1945 with a feeling of melancholy and, I suppose, something of uncertainty because I was saying good-by to an unforgettable era and I really had given very little thought to the fact that from this day forward I would be on my own.

I realized that in the future there would be many important changes in my way of living but I had long since realized that life is made up of a series of adjustments. If you have been married for forty years and if your husband has been President of the United States for a dozen years, you have made personal readjustments many times, some superficial, some fundamental. My husband and I had come through the years with an acceptance of each other's faults and foibles, a deep understanding, warm affection and agreement on essential values. We depended on each other. Because Franklin could not walk, I was accustomed to doing things that most wives would expect their husbands to do; the planning of the routine of living centered around his needs and he was so busy that I was obliged to meet the children's needs as well."

Eleanor moved on to her new life as a private citizen immediately upon FDR's death.

and had never used any of the fifty thousand dollars set aside for that purpose.

When Eleanor walked out of the White House on Friday for the last time, she waved to the reporters who had gathered to see her off. She climbed into the limousine that would take her to Union Station, where she boarded a train for New York City and her apartment in Washington Square. To the reporters waiting for her at her apartment, she said, "The story is over."[85] The woman who had not wanted

Although their marriage was never close, as a team Eleanor and Franklin spurred each other on to greater things than perhaps either could have accomplished individually.

to be the first lady had served in that position almost thirteen years, longer than any other first lady. Sixty-year-old Eleanor Roosevelt was a private citizen again.

Eleanor Assesses Her Situation

"I had few definite plans but there were certain things I did not want to do," Eleanor wrote in her autobiography.[86] She did not want to be in charge of a large household, to stop helping people, to grow old, or to live at Hyde Park. Franklin had left the mansion to her and then to the children for as long as they lived. At their deaths, it would go to the federal government. Knowing that it would become a presidential landmark, he had left a note suggesting that the family give it to the government to save the expense of

maintaining it. That solution was a relief to all of them.

In the first few months after Franklin's death, Eleanor had time to remember her marriage. As she wrote in *This I Remember:*

> He might have been happier with a wife who was completely uncritical. That I was never able to be and he had to find it in other people. Nevertheless, I think I sometimes acted as a spur, even though the spurring was not always wanted or welcome. I was one of those who served his purposes.[87]

Historian Lois Scharf concluded that Franklin also acted as a spur to Eleanor:

> She had indeed served his purposes, but he had also served hers. He furnished the stage upon which her incomparable abilities and human qualities could gain the widest audience and respect. Few Presidents and

no other First Ladies have ever used the platform to such effect. In less obvious ways he was her spur as much as she was his.[88]

As she recalled her partnership with Franklin, Eleanor reaffirmed her belief that he had been a great president in that he had accomplished much for his country and for the world.

Eleanor's friends had always given her more attention and affection than her husband and children had. She had maintained her earlier associations with Esther Lape, Lorena Hickok, Elinor Morgenthau, and Molly Dewson. As a private citizen, she could spend more time with them. Some of Eleanor's biographers, especially Blanche Wiesen Cook, claim that Eleanor's relationship with these women went beyond friendship to love, particularly with Hickok. While admitting that Eleanor was starved for affection, some of those who knew her well deny or at least question the rumors. One line of a letter Eleanor wrote Hickock supports this position: "I know you have a feeling for me which for one reason or another I may not return in kind."[89] Although their friendship took a different tack after that letter, they remained friends.

Her closest friend probably was Joe Lash, the young man she had met in 1939 when he was secretary of the American Student Union (ASU). She could confide in him her private thoughts and hopes. For Joe, Eleanor was a mentor, as he wrote in his diary, "She personifies my belief and faith in the possibility of the social democratic way instead of the communist."[90]

Because of Joe's earlier communist associations, he had testified before the House Un-American Activities Committee. J. Edgar Hoover, director of the Federal Bureau of Investigation (FBI), who did not like Eleanor, assigned FBI investigators to spy on Joe and Eleanor to see if she was having an affair with a communist. They even bugged her hotel room one time. They learned that she was trying to smooth the troubled love affair between Joe and Trude Pratt, whom he eventually married.

Eleanor with her physician, Dr. David Gurewitsch, and his wife in Leningrad. Eleanor and the Gurewitsches bought a New York City townhouse together.

Eleanor's Rating of Franklin's Presidency

After Franklin's death, Eleanor concluded that he had been a truly great president and that he had done much to improve life in the United States. In No Ordinary Time, *Doris Kearns Goodwin analyzes Eleanor's evaluation of Franklin as president.*

"Eleanor was convinced in the fall of 1945 that 'a new country is being born.' It seemed to her, she told her son Jimmy, that 'a giant transference of energy' had taken place between the president and the people. 'In the early days, before Pearl Harbor,' she said, 'Franklin was healthy and strong and committed to the Allied cause while the country was sick and weak and isolationist. But gradually, as the president animated his countrymen to the dangers abroad, the country grew stronger and stronger while he grew weaker and weaker, until in the end he was dead and the country had emerged more powerful and more productive than ever before.'

It was a romanticized view of her husband's leadership, ignoring the many fierce arguments they had had during the war regarding his decision to intern the Japanese Americans, his failure to do more to help the Jews of Europe, his surrender to big business on military contracts, his caution on civil rights. She had brooded over his shortcomings while he was alive, but now she could idealize him as she had idealized her father, and grasp the elements of his greatness—his supreme confidence, his contagious faith, his sense of timing, his political skills. Beneath all, there had been, she could now see, a fundamental commitment to humane and democratic values, a steadiness of purpose, a determination to win the war as fast as possible, a vision of the principles on which the peace would be based, a dedication to better the life of the average American."

Joe and Trude befriended Eleanor for as long as she lived, and he became one of her most knowledgeable biographers.

Eleanor's young personal physician, Dr. David Gurewitsch, became another close friend, as did his wife, Edna. Eventually Eleanor and the Gurewitsches bought a townhouse in New York City and remodeled it into two apartments for themselves.

For the first time in her life, Eleanor was on her own, but with the help of her friends, she was not alone. Her own work was not finished, and she needed to get back to her projects. The story was not over.

7 So Much to Do

Life has got to be lived!
—Eleanor Roosevelt

Since Eleanor had been active in public service for most of her adult life, retiring after Franklin's death did not even occur to her. She had some continuing projects and plans for a new one.

She returned to one of her favorite projects, writing "My Day," one week after Franklin's death. On April 18, 1945, she notified her readers that she would now be writing for herself as a private citizen, not as the president's wife. "My Day" became even more popular, as did her lec-

ture, radio, and television appearances. People respected her for taking a stand on issues, even if she stood alone. She sometimes belittled herself as a "fighter for unpopular causes."[91]

When Secretary of the Interior Ickes came to look over Hyde Park, which would be administered by his department, he tried to convince Eleanor to run for the U.S. Senate. "You will be unbeatable," he wrote her later.[92] Rumors were already circulating that she might run for vice-president under Truman. She declined without hesitation: "I want them [her children] to feel in the future that

Eleanor attends a UN meeting. The United Nations was Eleanor's pet project, begun before the end of World War II.

any running for public office will be done by them."[93] She did not want to compete with them or to influence their decisions to run for office.

Eleanor did want to concentrate on one new project, building peace in the world. As Joseph Lash remembered, "All through the war she had argued for a 'United Nations' rather than an Anglo-American approach to peacekeeping. In July, when the UN Charter was before the Senate, she had pleaded for its immediate ratification."[94] As far as she was concerned, the United Nations, established in 1942, was the greatest achievement of Franklin's presidency—and she wanted to help strengthen it. After Japan's surrender, Truman listed her as his first choice to serve as a delegate to the first meeting of the General Assembly of the United Nations in London in 1946.

Eleanor Joins the U.S. Delegation to the UN

The other four members of the United States delegation were men of stature in the federal government: James Byrnes, secretary of state; Edward Stettinius Jr., the U.S. member of the Security Council; Senator Tom Connally, chairman of the Senate Foreign Relations Committee; and Senator Arthur Vandenberg, senior Republican member of the Senate Foreign Relations Committee. The five alternates included John Foster Dulles, adviser to New York governor Thomas Dewey. The male delegates, the alternates, and their staffs rode to New York City on a special train and then to the departure pier in army limousines and buses, escorted by

police on motorcycles with lights flashing and sirens blaring. Eleanor, still wearing mourning black, went alone in a small car.

"She Can't Do Much Harm There!"

On board, Eleanor rose early and ate breakfast alone. Then she studied the stacks of State Department reports. On walks around the deck she talked with the other delegates. She attended every delegation meeting and all State Department interviews with the reporters on board. When the delegation arrived in London, Eleanor learned that the other four members had assigned her to Committee III, which was to deal with humanitarian, educational, and cultural problems. Knowing that the other delegates had been less than enthusiastic about her appointment, she was not surprised at her assignment:

> I could just see the gentlemen of our delegation puzzling over the list and saying: "Oh, no! We can't put Mrs. Roosevelt on the political committee. What could she do on the budget committee? Does she know anything about legal questions? Ah, here's the safe spot for her—Committee 3. She can't do much harm there!"[95]

Even before the UN Assembly concluded, the U.S. delegation had changed its mind about Eleanor. Joseph Lash reported about a lunch meeting of Dulles and Vandenberg: "They talked to each other, expressing amazement at Mrs. Roosevelt's good judgment. They really had not known her before, writing her off as an emotional, rattle-brained woman."[96]

Dulles asked her to speak in the General Assembly in response to Russia's demand for forced repatriation of refugees. Although she had no time to prepare a speech, Eleanor agreed because she knew that political refugees—those who had left their country because they disagreed with their government's policies—would probably be imprisoned or killed if they returned to their homelands. Without notes, she spoke calmly but forcefully about the need for all refugees to choose to return to their homelands or stay in another country. Never raising her voice, she countered every point that wily Russian Andrei Vishinsky had made. After both Vishinsky and she had finished defending their positions, the General Assembly voted and defeated Russia's proposal. Afterwards, as Eleanor wearily climbed the stairs at the hotel, she heard two voices behind her:

"Mrs. Roosevelt," one of them said, "we must tell you that we did all we could to keep you off the United States delegation. We begged the president not to nominate you. But now we feel we must acknowledge that we have worked with you gladly and found you good to work with. And we will be happy to do so again."[97]

Standing Alone

Instead of traveling so much, Eleanor thought that she might reach people by having a radio or television program. Her agent was not enthusiastic, as she tells in her autobiography.

"'You are too controversial a figure,' he told me. 'The sponsors would be afraid of you. Some of them feel so strongly about you that they believe the public would not buy any product on whose program you might appear.'

It is startling to realize that one is so deeply, fanatically disliked by a number of people. And yet, while I weigh as honestly as I can their grounds for disapproval, when I feel that I am right in what I do, it seems to me that I cannot afford, as a self-respecting individual, to refuse to do a thing merely because it will make me disliked or bring down a storm of criticism on my head. I often feel that too many Americans today tend to reject the thing, however right they believe it to be, that they want to do because they fear they will be unpopular or will find themselves standing alone instead of in the comfortable anonymity of the herd.

As a result, when I believe, after weighing the evidence, that what I am doing is right I go ahead and try as hard as I can to dismiss from my mind the attitude of those who are hostile. I don't see how else one can live."

Eleanor at an open meeting of the second session of the United Nations in Flushing Meadows, New York.

She didn't remember whether Dulles or Vandenberg made the apology.

The day after the first session of the United Nations concluded, Eleanor flew to Zilcheim, Germany, to see a refugee camp for the first time. She was sorely moved by the human misery she saw, especially that of a young boy:

> One boy of twelve wanted to sing for me. I was told that he had wandered into camp holding firmly by the hand his younger brother, who was about six. When he was asked for his name, he couldn't remember it. Nor did he know where he had lived nor who his parents were nor what had happened to them. He sang for me "A Song of Freedom" so touchingly that no one listening could speak.[98]

When President Truman was elected to a second term, he appointed Eleanor to a second term in the United Nations. She was getting busy with her own affairs again, but she accepted because she was convinced that only a forceful United Nations could bring peace to the world.

In 1946 the Human Rights Commission (Committee III) met in New York City with two objectives: to establish a permanent eighteen-nation Commission on Human Rights and to draft an international bill of rights. Eleanor was elected chairwoman of the commission. As Joseph Lash pointed out, everyone knew her ability: "She was a vigorous, businesslike, although always gracious, chairman."[99]

The Human Rights Commission took two years to define human rights. The eighteen members came from eighteen different nations with eighteen different cultures and eighteen different definitions of "human rights." When they fell behind their schedule, she insisted that they work fifteen hours a day. To one member who complained about the long hours, she implied that shorter speeches would bring shorter work days.

Finally, at 3:00 A.M. on December 10, 1948, the UN General Assembly voted to approve the Universal Declaration of Human Rights. Then, as one body, the delegates rose and gave Eleanor Roosevelt a standing ovation. Eventually published in the native language of every country in the United Nations, the Universal Declaration defines the rights of every person on the planet Earth. UN Secretary-General U Thant called it "The Magna Carta of Mankind."[100]

During the time that Eleanor was a delegate to the United Nations, she carried

Writing the Universal Declaration of Human Rights

During the working sessions, Russian delegate Dr. Alexei Pavlov delivered frequent long harangues of communist propaganda. Finally even Eleanor lost her patience. She tells the story in On My Own.

"Dr. Pavlov knew that most of us were getting tired of listening, but he began speaking again. He seemed likely to go on forever, but I watched him closely until he had to pause for breath. Then I banged the gavel so hard that the other delegates jumped in surprise and, before he could continue, I got in a few words of my own.

'We are here,' I said, 'to devise ways of safeguarding human rights. We are not here to attack each other's governments and I hope when we return on Monday the delegate of the Soviet Union will remember that!' I banged the gavel again. 'Meeting adjourned!'

I can still see Dr. Pavlov staring at me in surprise. But his orations were brief and to the point for about a week after that."

Eleanor holds the document she helped draft, the Universal Declaration of Human Rights.

on her personal work. She lectured 100 to 150 times a year, wrote her daily column for "My Day," and wrote the last two volumes of her autobiography. Her daily radio show and weekly television interview show were popular across the nation.

Eleanor Continues with Her Projects

Elected in 1952, President Dwight Eisenhower did not reappoint Eleanor to the United Nations. Still wanting to support the peace efforts of the United Nations, however, Eleanor joined the American Association for the United Nations (AAUN), a nongovernment volunteer group. In re-

sponse to requests from other countries, she became a goodwill ambassador, traveling as a private citizen and usually paying her own way. Circling the world, she toured many countries—some several times, talked with their leaders and their people, and lectured on peaceful relations.

In her travels Eleanor became particularly interested in Israel and went there often. Eleanor helped Israel generously. She gave fees for a lecture series to the United Jewish Appeal. Whenever in Israel, she always visited—and contributed to—a youth settlement named in her honor. To critics who questioned her attachment to Israel, she answered that Israel would show the Near East that democracy works.

Busy as she was with her world travels, Eleanor still found time to work for the

Her Next Project?

Joseph Lash, in Eleanor: The Years Alone, *describes Eleanor's quandary as she considered her future alone.*

"She still was looking for a job to do, groping for the assignment that would bring all her interests into a single focus. She had been deeply conscious during her White House years of how her energies had been scattered among a thousand enterprises. After Franklin's fourth-term election, Esther Lape had implored her to think over carefully the best ways to make use of the powers and opportunities that were so peculiarly hers. That involved a 'selection and decision,' Esther had cautioned her.

Now she was determined to do just that, and she was going to do the selecting. What she really wanted to do was to make some contribution to what had been Franklin's wartime objective—the establishment of machinery that would help ensure a lasting peace."

Still active, an elderly Eleanor chats with President John F. Kennedy in 1961.

Democratic Party. Candidates courted her favor, for her approval brought votes. Elected officials, including presidents, asked her advice. She aired her views on political issues: civil rights, nuclear disarmament, social problems. A main speaker at Democratic conventions, she always rated a standing ovation.

For years Eleanor had ignored the pleas of family and friends to slow down. Instead she took on more projects. In 1959, when she was seventy-five, she became a visiting lecturer at Brandeis University, where she had served on the board for years. Because she did not feel qualified, however, she would not accept the title of professor.

In 1962, when Eleanor was finishing her final book, *Tomorrow Is Now*, Dr. Gurewitsch diagnosed her "tired feeling" as a rare, untreatable blood disease. When she realized that her illness was terminal, she paid her semiannual contributions to various charities early so that they would not be short at Christmas. On October 11 family and friends gathered at her apartment for her seventy-eighth birthday party. On November 11, 1962, Eleanor Roosevelt died. She was buried beside Franklin in the rose garden at Hyde Park.

The Best Lesson

We can do it!

—Eleanor Roosevelt

In her last book, *Tomorrow Is Now*, Eleanor Roosevelt wrote, "Example is the best lesson there is."[101] Surely that statement is the key to her importance. Fully as influential as her managing and organizing skills was her ability to accomplish her goals. She did not just sit on the board of

Eleanor never stopped believing in human potential—that anyone could change the world.

the Red Cross canteens: She also mopped their floors. In expanding the position of the first lady, Eleanor strengthened her husband's presidency. Several subsequent first ladies, especially Rosalyn Carter and Hillary Rodham Clinton, named Eleanor as their role model.

Eleanor set an example for women when she championed feminist causes. When she was only nineteen, she tried to improve the working conditions of women. Later she tackled equal rights for women. An articulate speaker, hers was the voice not only for women but also for minorities, the economically deprived, child laborers, refugees, and the underprivileged.

Eleanor set an example for giving, for she was an incredibly generous woman. She gave all of the money she earned while Franklin was in office—and some years her income topped his—to various charities. Even after she was on her own, she included charities in her budget. Probably not even Eleanor knew how many people had asked her for help and received it. Aware that some might deceive her, she still believed that it was better to give to someone who did not need it than not to give to someone who did.

Other traits in her role model image were her accessibility—she rode city buses; her genuine concern for others—she lis-

Her Call for Leadership

In On My Own, *Eleanor considers the meaning of some of her travels.*

"The more I traveled throughout the world, the more I realized how important it is for Americans to see with understanding eyes the other peoples of the world whom modern means of communication and transportation are constantly making closer neighbors. Yet, the more I traveled, the happier I was that I happened to have been born in the United States, where there exist the concept of freedom and opportunities of advancement for individuals of every status. I felt, too, the great responsibility that has come, with our good fortune, to us as a people. The world is looking to us for leadership in almost every phase of development of the life of peoples everywhere. We had—we still have—the opportunity to live up to that call for leadership in a free world, and there has never been any doubt in my mind that we will live up to it."

tened just as intently to a beggar as she did to a king; and her gentle self-control —she never raised her voice. And she was an optimist—she had faith in people.

Eleanor's most far-reaching single contribution was her participation in the writing of the Universal Declaration of Human Rights for the United Nations. As chairman of the writing committee, she insisted that the document be written in simple language and that it protect every human being on earth. Like the U.S. Declaration of Independence, the Universal Declaration of Human Rights is not a legal paper, but a moral document.

Eleanor Roosevelt moved with ease and grace among royalty, heads of state, and the social elite; she moved with awareness and empathy among the hungry, the injured, and the homeless. Then she took steps to alleviate their situations. Without regard for race, color, nationality, sex, religion, economic status, or creed, she fulfilled her lifetime purpose: to improve the lot of humankind.

At the end of her life Eleanor was supremely confident about the future of humankind. In the book she finished just before her death, *Tomorrow Is Now*, she wrote, "This I know. This I believe with all my heart. If we want a free and a peaceful world, if we want to make the deserts bloom and man to grow to greater dignity as a human being—WE CAN DO IT!"[102]

Notes

Introduction: A Woman of Accomplishment

1. Blanche Wiesen Cook, *Eleanor Roosevelt*, vol. 1, 1884–1933. New York: Viking Penguin, 1992.
2. Quoted in Joseph P. Lash, *Eleanor: The Years Alone*. New York: W. W. Norton, 1972.
3. Quoted in Lash, *Eleanor: The Years Alone*.
4. Quoted in Helen Gahagan Douglas, *The Eleanor Roosevelt We Remember*. New York: Hill and Wang, 1963.
5. Quoted in Lash, *Eleanor: The Years Alone*.

Chapter 1: Eleanor's Painful Childhood

6. Eleanor Roosevelt, *The Autobiography of Eleanor Roosevelt*. New York: Harper & Brothers, 1961.
7. Quoted in Cook, *Eleanor Roosevelt*.
8. Roosevelt, *Autobiography*.
9. Roosevelt, *Autobiography*.
10. Roosevelt, *Autobiography*.
11. Roosevelt, *Autobiography*.
12. Roosevelt, *Autobiography*.
13. Roosevelt, *Autobiography*.
14. Roosevelt, *Autobiography*.
15. Roosevelt, *Autobiography*.
16. Quoted in Elliott Roosevelt and James Brough, *An Untold Story: The Roosevelts of Hyde Park*. New York: G. P. Putnam's Sons, 1973.
17. Roosevelt, *Autobiography*.

Chapter 2: The Emergence of Eleanor

18. Roosevelt, *Autobiography*.
19. Roosevelt, *Autobiography*.
20. Roosevelt, *Autobiography*.
21. Cook, *Eleanor Roosevelt*.
22. Roosevelt, *Autobiography*.
23. Quoted in Elliott Roosevelt, *An Untold Story*.
24. Roosevelt, *Autobiography*.
25. Roosevelt, *Autobiography*.
26. Quoted in Cook, *Eleanor Roosevelt*.
27. Quoted in Cook, *Eleanor Roosevelt*.
28. Roosevelt, *Autobiography*.
29. Cook, *Eleanor Roosevelt*.
30. Roosevelt, *Autobiography*.
31. Roosevelt, *Autobiography*.

Chapter 3: Independence at Last

32. Roosevelt, *Autobiography*.
33. Roosevelt, *Autobiography*.
34. Geoffrey C. Ward, *A First-Class Temperament: The Emergence of Franklin Roosevelt*. New York: Harper & Row, 1989.
35. Joseph P. Lash, *Eleanor and Franklin: The Story of Their Relationship Based on Eleanor Roosevelt's Private Papers*. New York: W. W. Norton, 1971.
36. Roosevelt, *Autobiography*.
37. Roosevelt, *Autobiography*.
38. Lash, *Eleanor and Franklin*.
39. Roosevelt, *Autobiography*.
40. Eleanor Roosevelt, *This I Remember*. New York: Harper & Brothers, 1949.
41. Roosevelt, *This I Remember*.
42. Roosevelt, *This I Remember*.
43. Roosevelt, *This I Remember*.
44. Quoted in Lorena A. Hickok, *Eleanor Roosevelt: Reluctant First Lady*. New York: Dodd, Mead, 1962.
45. Joseph P. Lash, *"Life Was Meant to Be Lived": A Centenary Portrait of Eleanor Roosevelt*. New York: W. W. Norton, 1984.
46. Quoted in Lash, *"Life Was Meant to Be Lived."*

Chapter 4: First Lady by Election, Not Choice

47. Quoted in Lash, *Eleanor and Franklin*.
48. Roosevelt, *This I Remember*.
49. Roosevelt, *This I Remember*.

50. Quoted in Maurine Beasley, ed., *The White House Press Conferences of Eleanor Roosevelt*. New York: Garland, 1983.

51. Quoted in Lash, *Eleanor and Franklin*.

52. Roosevelt, *This I Remember*.

53. Quoted in Lash, *Eleanor and Franklin*.

54. Quoted in Richard Harrity and Ralph G. Martin, *Eleanor Roosevelt: Her Life in Pictures*. New York: Duell, Sloan, and Pearce, 1958.

55. Quoted in Harrity and Martin, *Eleanor Roosevelt*.

56. J. William T. Youngs, *Eleanor Roosevelt: A Personal and Public Life*. Boston: Little, Brown, 1985.

57. Quoted in Youngs, *Eleanor Roosevelt*.

58. Quoted in Youngs, *Eleanor Roosevelt*.

59. Anna Eleanor Roosevelt, *It's Up to the Women*. New York: Frederick A. Stokes, 1933.

60. Roosevelt, *It's Up to the Women*.

Chapter 5: The Roosevelt Team

61. Quoted in Doris Kearns Goodwin, *No Ordinary Time: Franklin and Eleanor Roosevelt: The Home Front in World War II*. New York: Simon & Schuster, 1994.

62. Quoted in Lash, *Eleanor and Franklin*.

63. Roosevelt, *It's Up to the Women*.

64. Roosevelt, *It's Up to the Women*.

65. Eleanor Roosevelt, *If You Ask Me*. New York: D. Appleton–Century, 1946.

66. Quoted in Youngs, *Eleanor Roosevelt*.

67. Goodwin, *No Ordinary Time*.

68. Roosevelt, *Autobiography*.

69. Quoted in Goodwin, *No Ordinary Time*.

70. Quoted in Joan Hoff-Wilson and Marjorie Lightman, eds., *Without Precedent: The Life and Career of Eleanor Roosevelt*. Bloomington: Indiana University Press, 1984.

71. Quoted in Goodwin, *No Ordinary Time*.

72. Roosevelt, *This I Remember*.

73. Quoted in Goodwin, *No Ordinary Time*.

74. Quoted in Lash, *Eleanor and Franklin*.

75. Quoted in Roosevelt, *This I Remember*.

76. Quoted in Lash, *Eleanor and Franklin*.

77. Lash, *Eleanor and Franklin*.

78. Quoted in Lash, *Eleanor and Franklin*.

79. Quoted in Lash, *Eleanor and Franklin*.

80. Quoted in Lash, *Eleanor and Franklin*.

81. Roosevelt, *This I Remember*.

Chapter 6: Private Citizen Again

82. Roosevelt, *This I Remember*.

83. Quoted in Lash, *Eleanor and Franklin*.

84. Roosevelt, *This I Remember*.

85. Quoted in Goodwin, *No Ordinary Time*.

86. Roosevelt, *Autobiography*.

87. Roosevelt, *This I Remember*.

88. Quoted in Goodwin, *No Ordinary Time*.

89. Quoted in Goodwin, *No Ordinary Time*.

90. Quoted in Goodwin, *No Ordinary Time*.

Chapter 7: So Much to Do

91. Eleanor Roosevelt, *Tomorrow Is Now*. New York: Harper & Row, 1963.

92. Quoted in Lash, *Eleanor: The Years Alone*.

93. Quoted in Lash, *Eleanor: The Years Alone*.

94. Quoted in Lash, *Eleanor: The Years Alone*.

95. Eleanor Roosevelt, *On My Own*. New York: Harper & Brothers, 1958.

96. Lash, *Eleanor: The Years Alone*.

97. Roosevelt, *Autobiography*.

98. Roosevelt, *On My Own*.

99. Lash, *Eleanor: The Years Alone*.

100. Quoted in Youngs, *Eleanor Roosevelt*.

Epilogue: The Best Lesson

101. Roosevelt, *Tomorrow Is Now*.

102. Roosevelt, *Tomorrow Is Now*.

For Further Reading

Maurine H. Beasley, *Eleanor Roosevelt and the Media: A Public Quest for Self-Fulfillment*. Urbana: University of Illinois Press, 1987. Beasley describes how Eleanor learned to use the media—newspapers, magazines, radio, and television—to develop her projects and to earn a substantial income. Eleanor had a cordial relationship with media personnel, who generally liked her because she was punctual, knew what she was supposed to do, and was an unassuming colleague.

Peter Collier, *The Roosevelts: An American Saga*. New York: Simon & Schuster, 1994. Collier traces the two branches of the Roosevelt family—the Oyster Bay Roosevelts (Theodore's family) and the Hyde Park Roosevelts (Franklin's family). Eleanor linked the two clans. The author analyzes their personalities, ambitions, problems, successes, and failures.

Russell Freedman, *Eleanor Roosevelt: A Life of Discovery*. New York: Houghton Mifflin, 1933. This well-written biography for young adults highlights the main points of Eleanor's life but lacks documentation.

John Gunther, *Roosevelt in Retrospect: A Profile in History*. New York: Harper & Brothers, 1950. Although this book is primarily about Franklin, Gunther devotes a chapter to Eleanor and throughout the book describes the role she played in Franklin's life.

Stella K. Hershan, *The Candles She Lit: The Legacy of Eleanor Roosevelt*. Westport, CT: Praeger, 1993. This book, a sequel to Hershan's *A Woman of Quality*, tells of more people whom Eleanor helped. Also included is a brief biography of Eleanor.

Lorena A. Hickok, *The Story of Eleanor Roosevelt*. New York: Grosset & Dunlap, 1959. Since Hickok and Eleanor were friends, this book is an affectionate tribute to Eleanor for young readers.

Archibald MacLeish, *The Eleanor Roosevelt Story*. Boston: Houghton Mifflin, 1965. MacLeish supplies the text for this photographic biography of Eleanor from her birth to signing the Universal Declaration of Human Rights.

Alfred Steinberg, *Mrs. R: The Life of Eleanor Roosevelt*. New York: G. P. Putnam's Sons, 1958. Claiming to be the first full-length biography of Eleanor, this detailed book covers her life from birth to 1957.

Works Consulted

Maurine Beasley, ed., *The White House Press Conferences of Eleanor Roosevelt.* New York: Garland, 1983. This collection of Eleanor's answers to reporters' questions is not complete, but it gives the reader a sense of the subject matter they covered.

Blanche Wiesen Cook, *Eleanor Roosevelt,* vol. 1, 1884–1933. New York: Viking Penguin, 1992. Based on extensive research, this biography is detailed, thorough, and analytical. Cook probes into every nook of Eleanor's life, including the nature of her friendships with women.

Helen Gahagan Douglas, *The Eleanor Roosevelt We Remember.* New York: Hill and Wang, 1963. Having only praise and admiration for her friend Eleanor Roosevelt, Douglas includes some anecdotes involving both Eleanor and Franklin.

Eric Foner and John A. Garraty, eds., *The Reader's Companion to American History.* Boston: Houghton Mifflin, 1991. This book is a good quick-reference source for American history.

Doris Kearns Goodwin, *No Ordinary Time: Franklin and Eleanor Roosevelt: The Home Front in World War II.* New York: Simon & Schuster, 1994. Everything about this book is excellent: research, organization, documentation, analyses. Goodwin limits the time period to 1940–1945, although she summarizes Eleanor's contributions at the end of the book.

Richard Harrity and Ralph G. Martin, *Eleanor Roosevelt: Her Life in Pictures.* New York: Duell, Sloan, and Pearce, 1958. This pictorial biography, accompanied by text, covers Eleanor's life from birth to her years of world travel after her husband's death.

Stella K. Hershan, *A Woman of Quality.* New York: Crown, 1970. Hershan interviewed several people whom Eleanor had helped in some way. Their stories reveal Eleanor's concern and generosity.

Lorena A. Hickok, *Eleanor Roosevelt: Reluctant First Lady.* New York: Dodd, Mead, 1962. Hickok begins this biography with the Roosevelts' move into the White House. She describes their first two years there and ends with the account of a trip she and Eleanor took to the West—Yosemite Park, the California coast, and up to Oregon.

Joan Hoff-Wilson and Marjorie Lightman, eds., *Without Precedent: The Life and Career of Eleanor Roosevelt.* Bloomington: Indiana University Press, 1984. Thirteen scholars discuss Eleanor and her relationship to political history and women's history. Their combined essays give a full picture of Eleanor.

Joseph P. Lash, *Eleanor and Franklin: The Story of Their Relationship Based on Eleanor Roosevelt's Private Papers.* New York: W. W. Norton, 1971. Joseph Lash and Eleanor Roosevelt enjoyed a long-term, close friendship; his biographies of her have a deeper insight than those of most other writers. This book begins with the childhood of Eleanor and Franklin and ends with his death.

———, *Eleanor: The Years Alone.* New York: W. W. Norton, 1972. In this volume, Lash covers the years from Franklin's death to hers. An appendix chronicles the efforts to nominate her for the Nobel Peace Prize.

———, "Life Was Meant to Be Lived": A Centenary Portrait of Eleanor Roosevelt. New York: W. W. Norton, 1984. This one-volume, generously illustrated biography begins with her childhood and ends with her death.

———, Love, Eleanor: Eleanor Roosevelt and Her Friends. Garden City, NY: Doubleday, 1982. Lash weaves together excerpts from Eleanor's letters to and from friends with his comments.

Anna Eleanor Roosevelt, It's Up to the Women. New York: Frederick A. Stokes, 1933. She believed that "it's up to the women" to get the people through the depression.

Eleanor Roosevelt, The Autobiography of Eleanor Roosevelt. New York: Harper & Brothers, 1961. Eleanor wrote her autobiography in three volumes: This Is My Story (1937), This I Remember (1949), and On My Own (1958). In 1961 she condensed each volume somewhat and published them in this single comprehensive edition.

———, If You Ask Me. New York: D. Appleton–Century, 1946. This collection of questions asked of and answered by Eleanor is interesting, but absence of dates limits its use.

———, My Days. New York: Dodge, 1938. This book collects excerpts from Eleanor's newspaper column, "My Day." She honed her conversational writing style in these articles.

———, On My Own. New York: Harper & Brothers, 1958. Eleanor continued from Franklin's death to 1958.

———, This I Remember. New York: Harper & Brothers, 1949. This volume covers the period from Franklin's entry into politics until his death.

———, This Is My Story. New York: Harper & Brothers, 1937. This volume starts with her birth in 1884 and ends in 1924, when she and Franklin were moving back to New York City where he was to join a law firm.

———, Tomorrow Is Now. New York: Harper & Row, 1963. Completed just before her death, this book was published afterwards. She discussed her optimistic hopes for the future in the national and world economic situation, in education, in individual and world peace.

Elliott Roosevelt and James Brough, An Untold Story: The Roosevelts of Hyde Park. New York: G. P. Putnam's Sons, 1973. Elliott gives a more intimate view of his parents and their family life.

Geoffrey C. Ward, A First-Class Temperament: The Emergence of Franklin Roosevelt. New York: Harper & Row, 1989. This biography of Franklin includes some perceptive comments about Eleanor.

J. William T. Youngs, Eleanor Roosevelt: A Personal and Public Life. Boston: Little, Brown, 1985. This straightforward biography builds on facts but unfortunately does not include footnotes.

Interview

Nan Brooks, veteran actress who has taken her one-woman show, Dear Mrs. Roosevelt, on midwestern and national tours. June 27, 1995.

Index

Picture Credits

Cover photo: Archive Photos

Archive Photos/American Stock Photos, 45

FDR Library, 15, 20 (both), 23, 24, 27, 28 (both), 32, 36, 37, 39, 50, 53, 55, 61, 68, 75, 80, 83

Library of Congress, 16, 33, 40, 51, 52, 65, 70, 71

National Archives, 12, 26, 29, 30, 43, 49, 57, 60, 66, 69, 72 (both), 73, 74, 77, 81, 84

Stock Montage, Inc., 47

UN Photo, 10

UPI/Corbis-Bettmann, 13, 18, 41, 48, 63, 67

About the Author

A native Hoosier, Eileen Morey now lives in Bloomington, Indiana. Reading and photography take much of her time—and she's recently become addicted to browsing used bookstores.